XenServer Administration Handbook
Practical Recipes for Successful Deployments

Tim Mackey and J.K. Benedict

Beijing · Boston · Farnham · Sebastopol · Tokyo

XenServer Administration Handbook

by Tim Mackey and J.K. Benedict

Copyright © 2016 Tim Mackey and J.K. Benedict. All rights reserved.

Printed in the United States of America.

Published by O'Reilly Media, Inc., 1005 Gravenstein Highway North, Sebastopol, CA 95472.

O'Reilly books may be purchased for educational, business, or sales promotional use. Online editions are also available for most titles (*http://safaribooksonline.com*). For more information, contact our corporate/institutional sales department: 800-998-9938 or corporate@oreilly.com.

Editor: Nan Barber	**Indexer:** Angela Howard
Acquisitions Editor: Rachel Roumeliotis	**Interior Designer:** David Futato
Production Editor: Shiny Kalapurakkel	**Cover Designer:** Karen Montgomery
Copyeditor: Kim Cofer	**Illustrator:** Rebecca Demarest
Proofreader: Amanda Kersey	

March 2016:   First Edition

Revision History for the First Edition

2016-03-15:   First Release

See *http://oreilly.com/catalog/errata.csp?isbn=9781491935439* for release details.

978-1-491-93512-5

[LSI]

Table of Contents

Part II.   Management Recipes

Preface

With more than 150,000 organizations running XenServer virtualization in a production environment, it is easily one of the most popular platforms available for virtual machine (VM) management. Since its inception as a research project of the University of Cambridge in 2001, the core Xen Project hypervisor has consistently pushed the boundaries of data center computing. The XenServer technology was acquired from XenSource in 2007 by Citrix, and the technology has evolved to support high-density virtualization for both cloud and desktop workloads.

XenServer furthered its leadership role when, in 2013, Citrix partnered with NVIDIA to deliver true hardware graphics virtualization using NVIDIA GRID and XenServer to define a new class of virtual workload: the high-performance graphics workstation. Even more recently, this new type of virtual workload has been expanded to leverage both Intel and AMD video cards for Windows- and Linux-based Guest VMs.

This is the environment XenServer administrators are increasingly being called upon to optimize and manage. This book seeks to provide practical guidance for how to plan, deploy, operate, and troubleshoot a modern XenServer environment. Our goal is that regardless of whether you manage a modest installation of a few blades or multiple global enterprise data centers, if you've found XenServer to be a critical component of your organization, then there will be valuable content for the successful operation of your XenServer deployment.

How This Book Is Organized

To easily fulfill the goals of this book, namely providing administrators with the information they need to be successful with XenServer, we've organized the content into two parts.

Part 1 covers the content most valuable during the design phase of a deployment. This is where you'll find information on the architecture of XenServer, installation guidelines, best practices, and deployment blueprints. Some of the information in this portion of the book includes:

- Exactly what a "XenServer" is
- The critical components that make up a XenServer environment
- Installation of XenServer hosts
- Storage, network, and management paradigms

Part 2 covers day-to-day management information. Everything from log management through backup strategies are presented. The majority of the content in this section is provided in simple problem statements with easy resolutions. It's important to note that when resolutions are provided, the answer may include either XenCenter or command-line instructions. Most solutions will include the simplest path to resolution over presenting multiple solutions and going into detailed analysis of root causes.

Who This Book Is Written For

From seasoned "compile-it-from-scratch" Xen experts to college students maintaining a virtualized infrastructure in their spare time, this book was written with the specific purpose of making any XenServer administrator, experience aside, successful from installation to system-based lifecycle management.

No one person has ever climbed out of bed, headed into the office, and become a spontaneous XenServer administrator. Even we continue to learn from our colleagues and the Xen community; and we keep our own skills sharpened. It is this constant type of learning and problem solving that keeps us enthusiastic, driven, and energetic about XenServer's power to create an infrastructure. It is all this and more that, in turn, we have presented within these pages: something new or something familiar to ensure you have a successful XenServer deployment story to share with others.

Future Release Information

This book was specifically written to cover XenServer 6.5. At the time of its writing, XenServer Dundee was under development, and pre-release installers were publicly available. Some functionality is expected to be changing in Dundee, but there is no guarantee the pre-release changes won't be changed prior to final release. Where changes are known to exist in a preview form, we'll let you know.

About Us

At heart, we are absolute tech geeks. We both enjoy working with the latest technology while solving some pretty cool problems. When working with customers or users, we're both trying to find ways to quickly resolve whatever issue caused the customer or user to reach out for help. It is this passion for technology, coupled with an understanding for what it means to run software in production, that drove us to write this book. Put simply, we want every XenServer admin to be successful with XenServer, and this is one way to accomplish that goal.

Conventions Used in This Book

The following typographical conventions are used in this book:

Italic

> Indicates new terms, URLs, email addresses, filenames, and file extensions.

`Constant width`

> Used for program listings, as well as within paragraphs to refer to program elements such as variable or function names, databases, data types, environment variables, statements, and keywords.

`Constant width bold`

> Shows commands or other text that should be typed literally by the user.

`Constant width italic`

> Shows text that should be replaced with user-supplied values or by values determined by context.

 This element signifies a tip or suggestion.

 This element signifies a general note.

This element indicates a warning or caution.

Using Code Examples

This book is here to help you get your job done. In general, if example code is offered with this book, you may use it in your programs and documentation. You do not need to contact us for permission unless you're reproducing a significant portion of the code. For example, writing a program that uses several chunks of code from this book does not require permission. Selling or distributing a CD-ROM of examples from O'Reilly books does require permission. Answering a question by citing this book and quoting example code does not require permission. Incorporating a significant amount of example code from this book into your product's documentation does require permission.

We appreciate, but do not require, attribution. An attribution usually includes the title, author, publisher, and ISBN. For example: "*XenServer Administration Handbook* by Tim Mackey and J.K. Benedict (O'Reilly). Copyright 2016 Tim Mackey and Jesse Benedict, 978-1-4919-3543-9."

If you feel your use of code examples falls outside fair use or the permission given above, feel free to contact us at *permissions@oreilly.com*.

Safari® Books Online

 *Safari Books Online* is an on-demand digital library that delivers expert content in both book and video form from the world's leading authors in technology and business.

Technology professionals, software developers, web designers, and business and creative professionals use Safari Books Online as their primary resource for research, problem solving, learning, and certification training.

Safari Books Online offers a range of plans and pricing for enterprise, government, education, and individuals.

Members have access to thousands of books, training videos, and prepublication manuscripts in one fully searchable database from publishers like O'Reilly Media, Prentice Hall Professional, Addison-Wesley Professional, Microsoft Press, Sams, Que, Peachpit Press, Focal Press, Cisco Press, John Wiley & Sons, Syngress, Morgan Kaufmann, IBM Redbooks, Packt, Adobe Press, FT Press, Apress, Manning, New Riders,

McGraw-Hill, Jones & Bartlett, Course Technology, and hundreds more. For more information about Safari Books Online, please visit us online.

How to Contact Us

Please address comments and questions concerning this book to the publisher:

O'Reilly Media, Inc.
1005 Gravenstein Highway North
Sebastopol, CA 95472
800-998-9938 (in the United States or Canada)
707-829-0515 (international or local)
707-829-0104 (fax)

We have a web page for this book, where we list errata, examples, and any additional information. You can access this page at *http://bit.ly/xenserver_administration_hand-book*.

To comment or ask technical questions about this book, send email to *bookquestions@oreilly.com*.

For more information about our books, courses, conferences, and news, see our website at *http://www.oreilly.com*.

Find us on Facebook: *http://facebook.com/oreilly*

Follow us on Twitter: *http://twitter.com/oreillymedia*

Watch us on YouTube: *http://www.youtube.com/oreillymedia*

Acknowledgments

From Jesse

"What have I become, my Swedish friend?"

Trolle Selander, you brave man! I bow to both your impressive encouragement for chaotic (yet productive) scrums and courage in remaining my mentor, idol, and moral compass in wielding Hypervisor-specific code!

Mr. Mackey: XenServer Evangelist, Awesome Guy Extreme, and another brave mentor to myself. To think all of this could have changed if it hadn't been for our wonderful comrade and colleague Rachel Berry. I only recall that during my recovery from a long, long life of what the kids are mashing up as #DevOps and just trying to blend in, but NO! She was all too kind to pull me up and above the radar to introduce me to yourself and one Tobias Kreidl. In all seriousness (for once), I say to you, Bud: thank you for all you have done to encourage, push, collaborate, and challenge me as my evangelical mentor. I've seen less patience from pavement, Tim, and per my convenient tally, I believe I still owe you at *least* a pint?

Look, Dad, I made it to print, and as such, I further give my gratitude, respect, admiration, sarcastic disdain, and silent disagreements in EBCDIC format to Bill Aycock, Stead Halstead, Nick Kieffer, Tobias Kreidl, Ronald Lofton, Tim & John Martin, Sam McLeod, Todd Pigram, Varun & Deepika Sharma, Stephen Turner, and everyone from the "XenArchy Pod" to my colleagues around the world.

Lastly, I must express the gratitude I have for three special people whom—like my wife, Melissa—redefine what it means to be a *teacher*. They taught us so we would look beyond just the night's homework. They challenged us as so we would think outside of the classroom. They inspired us so we would find self-confidence and internal motivation. I thank you, Ellen Batchelder, Stephanie Pond-Lawler, and Elizabeth Ward (the self-proclaimed goddess of knowledge) for those lessons the three of you imprinted on us is—to this very day—still working its magic!

From Tim

The reality for me is that this book wouldn't be possible without the loyalty and endorsement XenServer has received from the user community at large. This loyalty to a product that I've come to be very closely associated with inspires me daily. I hope that I've been able to return that favor with some little nugget of goodness in here.

Over the years, I've been privileged to work on XenServer with a team of quite passionate people, the vast majority of whom have worked solidly behind the scenes. But I want to call attention to three key players: Tobias Kreidl, who is always willing to lend a hand to a fellow admin in need and is the most prolific support forum contributor; Steve Benton, who brought unwavering energy to the XenServer Masterclass; and Lee Bushen, who worked tirelessly preparing demo after demo for not only the XenServer Masterclass, but for the Masterclass Extra. If you were lucky enough to be a participant in one of those Masterclass events, you'll remember how we "don't stop until you drop"—a reference to the Masterclass continuing so long as attendees were asking questions, even if it were hours after the scheduled end of the event.

Lastly, I want to thank everyone who either reviewed the content for this book or contributed ideas for it. Without you, there wouldn't be a book, and your efforts do not go unnoticed.

Oh, and Jesse, I'll collect on that pint someday and probably buy a few myself.

Designing a Successful XenServer Deployment

XenServer is a powerful virtualization platform that in its most recent release is capable of officially hosting 1,000 virtual machines (VMs) with close to 100 of those being graphics-intensive, workstation-class VMs. This level of scalability is inherent to the platform, but being able to achieve such levels of virtualization requires some planning. In this part of the book, we'll be covering core concepts every administrator should be aware of when working with XenServer. Many of the topics covered are fairly detailed, but we're going to keep the information very admin-specific and not go deep into items an engineer developing XenServer might deal with.

After all, this is the administrators handbook, and you should expect actionable information!

We are going cover precisely what a XenServer is, what it is not, its origins, what makes it work, where to look for core configuration items. In addition, we'll provide specific guidance on issues that directly impact deployments. Much of what is covered could be considered best practice, but we're going to steer away from that term and simply call it practical advice.

Before we continue, it is important for us to remind you that when in doubt, please do consult the XenServer Administrator's Guide (*http://support.citrix.com/article/CTX141500*) for the specific version of XenServer you are working with. Documentation, features, release notes, and many other important resources for the version of XenServer you are planning to deploy can be accessed any time at *http://support.citrix.com*.

## CHAPTER 1

What Is a XenServer?

The answer to this simple question is, "XenServer is a pre-packaged Xen-based virtualization solution." Unfortunately, while an equally simple response, for many it doesn't answer the core question, so let's dive a bit deeper into what a XenServer is.

Quite a few years ago, both of us had made decent livings writing code. Some of the projects were rather substantial and were used in highly regulated industries, while others were a bit more modest. Regardless of the scope, we both found it important to ensure there was understanding of the solution being delivered. Where confusion over the project would arise, it was always imperative to provide answers to any questions posed. After all, user expectations go a long way to follow on sales and greater adoption.

Unfortunately for XenServer, there is a bit of inherent confusion out there. For years, we both have heard people who want XenServer, but refer to it as "Xen" and occasionally as "a Xen Server." While some of those people aren't in a technical position, when they need answers to a burning question, it's important to get them the right answer quickly.

As an example, if someone is working on a project that they want to integrate with XenServer, it does them no good to look at resources describing how "Xen" works. While the two technologies are definitely related, the right answer for "Xen" might be the wrong answer for "XenServer," and knowing the difference between these is key for any XenServer administrator.

Sure, we now know that "XenServer is a pre-packaged Xen-based virtualization solution" built around the Xen Project, but this is merely the beginning, as now we need to explain what Xen is, what it does, and how it forms the complete XenServer solution for which you will be responsible.

Future Development

At the time this book was written, early access to a potential future version of XenServer was available. This version code named "Dundee" contained changes to several core XenServer features. In the event a topic that is known to be different in Dundee is presented, this fact is called out in a box like this one labeled "Dundee Changes."

The Xen Hypervisor

The Xen hypervisor forms the core of all Xen-based virtualization platforms and, like VMware ESXi and Microsoft Hyper-V, is a "bare metal" hypervisor. This means that the first code that starts on the machine is the hypervisor and that a general-purpose operating system isn't required to manage the system.

What Is a Hypervisor? What Is Virtualization?

A hypervisor is a virtual machine manager (VMM) that uses a combination of hardware or software technologies to virtualize, or run, multiple operating environments at the same time. Basically, you can run many operating systems on top of the same hardware.

Originally designed at the University of Cambridge in Cambridge, England, Xen forms the core hypervisor in not only XenServer but also Oracle VM and can be used as an optional hypervisor within major Linux distributions such as CentOS, Debian, and SUSE Linux Enterprise Server. Additionally, Xen has been heavily used with what is arguably the most famous deployment at Amazon: providing the basis of its Amazon Web Services product offering.

Xen is actively developed under stewardship within the Xen Project: a Linux Foundation Collaborative Project, where it benefits from the active participation and contributions of well over a dozen organizations. This breadth of development ensures that the Xen hypervisor technology keeps pace with changing trends in data center operations while remaining focused on delivering hypervisor services.

Along with the depth of development put into the Xen hypervisor, it's important to note that each Xen-based product chooses which version of the Xen hypervisor to support and which features of that version to integrate. As such, it's common for some hypervisor features present in Xen to not be utilized in other packaged solutions.

About the Xen Project

The Xen Project is a collaborative project of the Linux Foundation. It was created when Citrix decided the core Xen technology it had acquired from XenSource would benefit from independent governance and stewardship. The Xen Project encompasses many subprojects, with both the Xen hypervisor and the XAPI toolstack being used within XenServer. You can learn more about the Xen Project and all subprojects at *http://www.xenproject.org/*.

Tooling for Xen Virtualization

The Xen hypervisor simply performs virtual machine management and needs some form of tooling to control its operation. Modern tooling options include *libvirt*, a library for virtualization management, and XAPI, the Xen management API. When implementing a customized Xen-based solution, you are free to choose the tooling that best suits your needs. However, because XenServer is a packaged Xen virtualization solution, the tooling has been chosen for you and that is the XAPI toolstack.

Toolstack: No Trading!

The XAPI toolstack is integral to the XenServer virtualization solution and cannot be swapped out for another Xen hypervisor management stack. As such, the scope of this book focuses on the XAPI toolstack, associated daemons, and the expansive xe command-line suite of utilities.

XAPI provides interfaces and implementations for all expected functions of VM operations, host management, storage, and networking configuration. Also, where two or more XenServer hosts are pooled together, XAPI provides additional controls over this type of resource pool and its operations. For those familiar with libvirt, XAPI is able to manage multiple hosts as an aggregate and is functionally similar to libvirt with some oVirt extensions. Lastly, we should not forget that XAPI exposes its API to some of the most popular DevOps languages in use, such as Java, JavaScript, PowerShell, Python, and C++.

## CHAPTER 2

Core Architecture and Critical Components

In Chapter 1, we stated that "XenServer is a pre-packaged, Xen-based virtualization solution." This implies that anyone with sufficient skill can re-create XenServer by starting with the Xen hypervisor. In reality, there is a rather large number of decisions anyone embarking on this task must make, and thankfully the team at Citrix has already made the bulk of those decisions. In this chapter, we'll cover the core components that make up a production XenServer deployment.

XenServer Isn't Linux, but dom0 Is

The misconception that XenServer is Linux is easily arrived at because from installation to privileged user space access, everything looks, feels, and tools much like a standard Linux environment. The boot loader used is `extlinux`, and the installer uses a familiar dialog for interactive setup and post installation. The administrator ends up within a Linux operating system logged in as the privileged user named root.

Post installation, when the Xen hypervisor starts, it is instantiating a privileged VM known as the control domain or, as it is commonly referred to, dom0. This control domain is a Linux VM with a custom kernel and a modified CentOS base with a very small footprint. From an administrative point of view, dom0 can be seen as a true, highly privileged VM that is responsible for core operations within Xen-based virtualization.

Control Domain and dom0

Throughout this book, reference to the privileged software layer that facilitates virtualization of VMs will be referred to as either the control domain or dom0. While both are technically correct to describe the post-boot environment you will administer, it is more important to state that both of these terms are identifiers used interchangeably throughout the XenServer virtualization solution.

If you're familiar with Linux-based systems running open source virtualization solutions, such as CentOS with KVM installed, your first instinct may likely be to log in: attempting to configure the XenServer installation within the control domain. You might also expect that XenServer will automatically accept any Linux style configuration changes you make to core items like storage and networking. And for those of you who have worked with VMware vSphere in the past, this Linux environment may appear similar to the service console.

The point we are making here is that while XenServer isn't Linux, and dom0 is, being a Linux expert is not a requirement. Rarely will changes to Linux configuration files inside of dom0 be required, and we want to guide you away from making your administrative life any more complicated than it needs to be. The control domain for XenServer has a very rich command-line interface; and where changes may be needed, they will be discussed within this book.

For those of you who are familiar with Linux, you might encounter situations where commands and packages appear to be missing. As an example, if you try to execute yum update, you'll quickly find that the repository *yum* points to is empty. It might then become tempting to point the *yum* package management utility at an upstream CentOS or EPEL (Extra Packages for Enterprise Linux) software repository.

Why yum Is Disabled

The XenServer control domain is highly customized to meet the needs of a virtualization platform, and as a result, installation of packages not explicitly designed or certified for XenServer could destabilize or reduce scalability and performance of the XenServer host. In the event host operations aren't impacted, when a XenServer update or upgrade is installed, it should be expected that any third-party or additional packages might break or be completely removed and that configuration changes made to files XenServer isn't explicitly aware of could be overwritten.

Now, with these warnings out of the way, here are the Linux operations that are perfectly safe in a XenServer environment:

Issuing any XenServer xe *command*

If the command is issued as part of a script, be sure to back up that script because a XenServer update might overwrite or remove it. Throughout this book, we'll provide instructions based on xe commands.

Interactively running any Linux command that queries the system for information

It's important to note that some commands might have richer XenServer equivalents. A perfect example of this is top. While this utility is available as part of the user space in XenServer, the information it provides is only reflective of Linux processes running in dom0; not virtual machine or physical host statistics. The utility xentop is a XenServer equivalent that provides richer information on the running user VMs in the system, and is also executed from dom0. Throughout this book, you'll see references to extended commands that, as an administrator, you'll find solve specific tasks.

Directly modifying configuration files that XenServer explicitly tracks

A perfect example of such a configuration file is */etc/multipath.conf*. Because dom0 is a CentOS distribution, it also contains support for the majority of the same devices an equivalent CentOS system would. If you wish to connect iSCSI storage in a multipath manner, you will likely need to modify */etc/multipath.conf* and add in hardware-specific configuration information.

Architecture Interface

Because XenServer isn't Linux, but dom0 is, what are the core interfaces within a XenServer environment? For that we need a diagram; see Figure 2-1. In this diagram, we see three main hardware elements: compute, network, and storage. Each of the lines represents how access is maintained. The first software element is the hypervisor. It is loaded from local storage and interfaces with compute to provide virtual machine services.

The first virtual machine is dom0, and as has already been discussed, dom0 is a privileged domain. Unprivileged domains are known as domU, or more simply, "Guest VMs," "guests," or just "VMs." All domains are controlled by the hypervisor, which provides an interface to compute services. VMs, of course, need more than just compute, so dom0 provides access to the hardware via Linux device drivers. The device driver then interfaces with a XenServer process, thus providing a virtual device interface using a split-driver model. The interface is called a split-driver model because one portion of the driver exists within dom0 (the backend), while the remainder of the driver exists in the guest (the frontend).

This device model is supported by processes including the Quick Emulator (QEMU) project. Because HVM and PVHM guests (discussed in Chapter 6) do not contain para-virtualization (PV) drivers, QEMU and QEMU-dm emulate aspects of hardware components, such as the BIOS, in addition to providing network and disk access.

QEMU

You can find more information regarding the QEMU project at *http://wiki.qemu.org*.

Finally, tying everything together is a toolstack, which for XenServer is also from the Xen Project and is called XAPI.

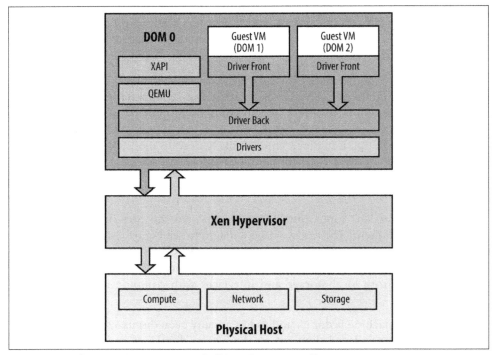

Figure 2-1. The main components of all XenServer installations

XenCenter: A Graphical Xen Management Tool

Once a XenServer host is installed, it can be managed immediately via Secure Shell (SSH) access to the command-line interface (CLI). Additionally, XenServer can also be managed by using XenCenter, a Windows-based, graphical interface for visualization and video terminal access to one or more XenServer hosts (Figure 2-2).

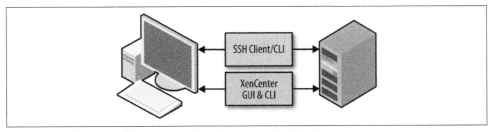

Figure 2-2. Command line or graphically: managing XenServer

XenCenter provides a rich user experience to manage multiple XenServer hosts, resource pools, and the entire virtual infrastructure associated with them. While other open source and commercial tools exist to manage XenServer, XenCenter is specifically designed in parallel with each XenServer release. XenCenter takes user credentials and then interacts with XenServer using the XenAPI.

XenCenter is designed to be backward compatible with legacy XenServer versions, which means best practice is to always use the most recent XenCenter available. If you require the specific version of XenCenter that shipped with the XenServer software installed on a given host, you can obtain it by opening a web browser and entering the IP address of your XenServer host.

Core Processes

The core processes of a XenServer are what differentiates XenServer from other Xen based distributions or from other implementations of dom0 that might exist. Each of the following core processes either implement a key feature of XenServer, are responsible for its scalability, or are critical to its security.

XAPI

XAPI is the core toolstack interface and exposes the Xen management API. It is responsible for the coordination of all operations across a XenServer environment and interfaces directly with most critical components.

XAPI also responds to HTTP requests on port 80 to provide access to download the XenCenter installer.

Log data relevant to XAPI can be found in either */var/log/xensource.log* or */var/log/audit.log*. These logs are particularly relevant when administrative tools, such as XenCenter, use XAPI to manage XenServer infrastructure.

xhad

xhad is the XenServer High Availability (HA) daemon. It is automatically started if the XenServer host is in a pool that has HA enabled on it. This process is responsible for all heartbeat activities and exchanges heartbeat information with other member servers to determine which hosts have definitely failed due to watchdog timer failure and subsequent host fencing.

High Availability

It is strongly recommended that a XenServer deployment utilizing HA should have at least three XenServer hosts within a pooled configuration. While it is possible to enable HA with two hosts, heartbeat priority will be based on the XenServer host unique identifier.

Because XAPI is a critical component of operation, xhad serves as a XAPI watchdog when HA is enabled. If XAPI appears to have failed, then xhad will restart it. HA should always be configured via XAPI commands, and the resultant configuration will be stored on each host in */etc/xensource/xhad.conf*.

Log data relevant for xhad can be found on dom0 in */var/log/xha.log*.

xenopsd

The Xen Operations daemon, xenopsd, is responsible for managing the life of a Guest VM while providing separation between management (XAPI) and virtualization processes (Xen). As a Guest VM is created or started, a xenopsd process is spawned: responsible for managing low-level tasks for that Guest VM such as resource manipulation and the collection of resource usage statistics for dom0.

Log data relevant to xenopsd can be found in */var/log/xensource.log*.

xcp-rrdd

xcp-rrdd is a daemon that is designed to receive and submit data in a round-robin fashion, which is then stored in a round-robin database. This daemon receives metrics from xenopsd regarding resource usage of Guest VMs. Examples of such statistics are disk IOPS, CPU load, and network usage. Where XenServer's NVIDIA GRID GPU or vGPU pass-through technology is used, metrics for these workloads are also collected. This information is then distributed back to the administrator—on request, such as with XenCenter—for viewing both current and historical performance for Guest VMs.

Log data relevant to xcp-rrdd can be found in both */var/log/xcp-rrdd-plugins.log* and */var/log/xensource.log*.

xcp-networkd

This daemon is responsible for the monitoring and reporting of XenServer network interfaces, such as the virtual bridged network.

SM

SM is the storage manager and is responsible for mapping supported storage solutions into XAPI as storage repositories, plugging virtual storage devices into storage repositories, and handling storage operations like storage migration and snapshots.

Log data relevant to the storage manager can be found in */var/log/SMlog*.

perfmon

Perfmon is a daemon that tracks dom0 performance and statistics.

mpathalert

mpathalert sends notifications to XenCenter, or another management interface polling for XAPI messages, when storage issues related to multipathing occur. This is a useful tool to troubleshoot networking issues for specific storage types and to also prevent single points of failure, such as where one path is down and is not coming back online.

Log data relevant to mpathalert can be found in */var/log/daemon.log* and */var/log/ messages*.

snapwatchd

The snapwatchd daemon is responsible for calling, monitoring, and logging for processes related to VM snapshots. Information such as the virtual disk state is kept in sync, allowing XAPI to track any changes in a Guest VM's disk or associated snapshots.

Log data relevant to snapwatchd can be found in */var/log/SMlog*.

stunnel

stunnel, or the secure tunnel, is used to encrypt various forms of traffic between real or virtual points by using Open SSL. Client connections to Guest VMs, such as vncterm access through XenCenter, leverage stunnel to ensure these types of sessions are kept separate and secure.

Log data relevant to stunnel can be found in */var/log/secure* and */var/log/ xensource.log*.

xenconsoled

The recording and logging of console-based activity, inclusive of guest and control domain consoles, is handled by xenconsoled.

Log data relevant to xenconsoled can be found in */var/log/xen/* or */var/log/ daemon.log*.

xenstored

The xenstored daemon is a database that resides in dom0. It provides low-level operations, such as virtual memory, shared memory, and interfaces with XenBus for general I/O operations. The XenBus provides a device abstraction bus similar to PCI that allows for communication between Guest VMs and dom0. Device drivers interact with the xenstored configuration database to process device actions such as "power-off" or "reboot" resulting from VM operations.

Log data relevant to xenstored can be found in */var/log/xenstored-access.log*, */var/log/ messages*, and */var/log/xensource.log*.

squeezed

squeezed is the dom0 process responsible for dynamic memory management in Xen-Server. XAPI calls squeezed to determine if a Guest VM can start. In turn, squeezed is responsible for interfacing with each running Guest VM to ensure it has sufficient memory and can return host memory to XenServer should a potential overcommit of host memory be encountered.

Log data relevant to squeezed can be found in */var/log/xensource.log*, */var/log/ xenstored-access.log*, and depending on your XenServer version, */var/log/squeezed.log*.

Critical Configuration Files

During host startup, dom0 uses init scripts and XAPI to validate its configuration. This ensures that a XenServer can return to a known valid configuration state following a host outage, such as a restart or recovery from a loss of power. If Linux configuration files have been manually modified by an administrator, it's not uncommon for XAPI to overwrite those changes from its configuration database.

Modification of Critical Configuration Files

In this section of the book, the files and directories listed are for administrative purposes only. Unless specified, do not modify or alter the directories and/or contents.

As a failsafe mechanism, if configuration fails the sanity checks, dom0 will boot into maintenance mode, and VMs will not start. Should this occur, administrative intervention will be required to correct the issue and bring the host back online. This model ensures a healthy system and validates the integrity of the physical host, virtual machine data, and associated storage.

/boot/extlinux.conf

The bootloader used by XenServer 6.5 is extlinux: a derivative of the Syslinux Project specifically geared toward booting kernels stored on EXT-based filesystems. Example 2-1 shows a default configuration of the kernel boot.

This configuration file provides instructions, based on a label convention, as to which kernel configuration should be loaded along with additional parameters once the physical hardware has been powered on. The default label (or kernel definition) used to load XenServer will always be flagged under the xe label.

Example 2-1. Example of the default XenServer kernel boot configuration

```
label xe
    # XenServer
    kernel mboot.c32
    append /boot/xen.gz mem=1024G dom0_max_vcpus=2
    dom0_mem=2048M,max:2048M watchdog_timeout=300
    lowmem_emergency_pool=1M crashkernel=64M@32M
    cpuid_mask_xsave_eax=0 console=vga vga=mode-0x0311
    --- /boot/vmlinuz-2.6-xen root=LABEL=rootenhlwylk ro
    xencons=hvc console=hvc0 console=tty0 quiet vga=785 splash
    --- /boot/initrd-2.6-xen.img
```

Additionally, kernel configurations are also offered for serial console access, or xe-serial, as well as a safe kernel, or safe, as shown in Example 2-2. These can be accessed during the initial boot sequence by entering menu.c32 when prompted by the boot: prompt.

Example 2-2. Alternate kernels

```
label xe-serial
    # XenServer (Serial)
    kernel mboot.c32
    append /boot/xen.gz com1=115200,8n1 console=com1,vga
    mem=1024G dom0_max_vcpus=2 dom0_mem=2048M,max:2048M
    watchdog_timeout=300 lowmem_emergency_pool=1M
    crashkernel=64M@32M cpuid_mask_xsave_eax=0 ---
    /boot/vmlinuz-2.6-xen root=LABEL=root-enhlwylk ro
    console=tty0 xencons=hvc console=hvc0 ---
    /boot/initrd-2.6-xen.img

label safe
    # XenServer in Safe Mode
    kernel mboot.c32
    append /boot/xen.gz nosmp noreboot noirqbalance acpi=off
    noapic mem=1024G dom0_max_vcpus=2 dom0_mem=2048M,max:2048M
    com1=115200,8n1 console=com1,vga ---
    /boot/vmlinuz-2.6-xen nousb root=LABEL=root-enhlwylk ro
    console=tty0 xencons=hvc console=hvc0 ---
    /boot/initrd-2.6-xen.img
```

Dundee Changes

The preview release of XenServer Dundee uses GRUB2 as its bootloader.

/etc/hosts

The *hosts* file is specifically populated so that specific dom0 processes can resolve to any of the following entries within the *hosts* file:

- localhost
- localhost.localdomain
- 127.0.0.1

The following command allows you to view the contents of the *hosts* file:

```
# cat /etc/hosts
127.0.0.1 localhost localhost.localdomain
```

/etc/hostname

The *hostname* file contains the distinct name for the host that was provided during installation. This file is only relevant to the control domain unless it is on record within the infrastructure's DNS (Domain Name Service).

As an example, the `hostname` can be `xenified01` and stored as such in */etc/hostname*:

```
# cat /etc/hostname
xenified01
```

However, in XenCenter this host can be given a friendly name, such as XENHOST1 for visual purposes, as shown in Figure 2-3.

Figure 2-3. The host's name can remain the same while showing a friendly name within XenCenter

/etc/multipath.conf

Many storage devices offer the ability for a host, such as XenServer, to leverage multiple paths or I/O channels for storage purposes. XenServer supports storage configurations that use multiple paths. This support is provided via device mapper multipathing (DM-MP), and the configuration information is stored in */etc/multipath.conf*. The default */etc/multipath.conf* file covers a wide range of modern storage devices ensuring XenServer hosts may utilize storage redundancy, failover, and aggregation for supported storage solutions.

Do Not Alter multipath.conf Without Guidance

While dom0 make look like a standard CentOS distribution, modifying *multipath.conf* following Linux examples found on the Internet can easily adversely impact system stability and performance. Always modify *multipath.conf* under the guidance of Citrix technical support or your hardware vendor.

/etc/resolv.conf

The *resolve.conf* file contains DNS entries for XenServer that were specified during installation (discussed in Chapter 3) or changed via XenCenter or XAPI command.

While this file can be manually modified for troubleshooting name resolution issues, on reboot, the XAPI configuration will overwrite any modifications made to this file in an effort to retain valid DNS server settings configured via XenCenter or through the xe command-line tool.

/etc/iscsi/initiatorname.iscsi

Open-iSCSI is installed to facilitate storage connections that use iSCSI-based technology. During an install, a unique iSCSI Qualified Name (IQN) is generated for each XenServer host and is stored, per XenServer host, in */etc/iscsi/initiatorname.iscsi*.

As an administrator trying to lock down iSCSI storage for specific hosts, the IQN can be determined per XenServer host, as shown in Example 2-3.

Example 2-3. Finding the XenServer's IQN

```
# cat /etc/iscsi/initiatorname.iscsi
InitiatorName=iqn.1994-05.com.redhat:dc785c10706
```

The output provides the IQN, and this can then be added to the initiator white list on the storage device. If a reinstall of XenServer is done, this value will change and all iSCSI hosts will need to have their white lists updated with the new, randomly generated IQN.

/etc/xensource/

In line with standard Linux convention, many "config" files related to Xen, Xen-Server, and other core XAPI processes are stored here. The majority of these files are generated on installation, updated from Xen-based tools, and in some cases, created when a XenServer administrator enabled a given feature.

boot_time_cpus

This is populated on each boot and contains information regarding the physical host's socket and cores-per-socket information. For Linux users, if this seems familiar, it is a dump of cpuinfo that is found in the */proc/* runtime filesystem. Example 2-4 shows the command to view the contents of the *boot_time_cpus* file. This information is not only saved in this file but also known by dom0. In turn, the XAPI database is updated with this information and propagated to peers where the host is a member in a XenServer pool.

Example 2-4. View boot_time_cpus

```
# cat /etc/xensource/boot_time_cpus
```

To compare the accuracy of this file against dom0's Linux-based */proc/* filesystem (populated at runtime), issue the command listed in Example 2-5.

Example 2-5. Checking for CPU information and its accuracy

```
# diff /etc/xensource/boot_time_cpus /proc/cpuinfo
```

The normal output should be nothing, or that no difference exists between */proc/cpuinfo* and */etc/xensource/boot_time_cpus*. As the former is generated by dom0 after the host boots and the Xen kernel begins its boot processes, any difference between these files would be an indication of a serious misconfiguration.

/etc/xensource/bugtool/

The *bugtool* directory has a few subdirectories and XML files, which define scope, attributes, and limits for data output as it relates to XenServer's built-in bugtool. Such files dictate tools, maximum output size, and other criteria necessary for the crash dump kernel (or server status report) to access, exploit, and store data needed under erroneous conditions.

/etc/xensource/db.conf

This file, along with a slightly longer version named *db.conf.rio*, describes the following XenServer database configuration information:

- Where to find the XAPI database
- The format to use when reading the database
- Sanity information relating to session usage and validity

/etc/xensource/installed-repos/

The *installed-repos* directory contains subdirectories that, either from a fresh installation or upgrade, list the repositories used during installation of the host. If supplemental packs are installed, they will also be listed under *installed-repos*; and upon upgrade, you will be alerted to the presence of the supplemental pack. This ensures that if an installation is dependent upon a specific supplemental pack, during upgrade, an administrator can verify and obtain a suitable replacement.

/etc/xensource/master.d/

This directory can contain one or more init-level scripts that were used during host initialization. In addition, an example init-level script is provided and for XenServer administrators is a good reference illustrating the flow of run-level activities, initialization sequencing, and resources called. This example script should be named *01-example*, but if one is not present on your system, this is OK.

Dundee Changes

XenServer Dundee has a control domain that is based on CentOS 7. CentOS 7 has adopted the `systemd` model for initialization. This model differs greatly in how init-level scripts are executed. If you have installed any management agents or custom scripts, please be aware they may not function in a `systemd` environment as they did previously.

/etc/xensource/network.conf

The *network.conf* file describes to the administrator what type of virtual network fabric is being used by a XenServer host. Example 2-6 shows the command to view this file. There are two syntactical options: `bridge` or `openvswitch`. `bridge` corresponds to the legacy Linux network bridge, while `openvswitch` corresponds to the Open Virtual Switch or `ovs`. The `ovs` is the default network used for all installations starting with XenServer 6.0, but if an older system is upgraded, then the Linux bridge may still be in place. It's important to note that new network functionality will only be developed for the `ovs`, while at some point, the Linux bridge may be retired.

Example 2-6. View network.conf

```
# cat /etc/xensource/network.conf
```

The output will either state "*bridge*" or "*openvswitch*," but this is a powerful piece of information to have—especially in diagnosing XenServer pool issues where the virtual network fabric, or "backend networking," is in question. Furthermore, there are some third-party Citrix products that may require that the virtual networking fabric is of one type or another. If it is found that a particular host needs to have its virtual network fabric switched, ensure all Guest VMs are halted (or migrated to another XenServer host), and issue the command listed in Example 2-7.

Example 2-7. Change network backend

```
# xe-switch-network-backend {bridge | openvswitch}
```

The host should reboot, and upon reboot will be conducting network operations via the mode specified.

/etc/xensource/pool.conf

Another key file for troubleshooting, *pool.conf* is used to determine if a host is a standalone server, pool master (primary), or slave (pool member reporting to a primary XenServer). The file can have one of two values: *master* or *slave.*

Using the `cat` command, as illustrated in Example 2-8, one can determine from the contents of *pool.conf* if the XenServer host thinks it is a pool master or a pool slave/member.

Example 2-8. Determine host role

```
# cat /etc/xensource/pool.conf
```

If the result of the command is `master`, then the host has the role of pool master. If the result of the command includes the word `slave`, the host is a member server and the IP address of the pool master will also be provided. When working with a standalone XenServer host (i.e., one not part of a pool), the standalone host will assume the role of `master`.

Only in the event of serious configuration corruption should this file be manually edited, and then only under guidance from the XenServer support team. Examples of such corruption include:

- High Availability being enabled when it should be disabled, such as during maintenance mode
- A network communication problem among pool members
- dom0 memory exhaustion
- Timeout induced by latency when electing a new pool master
- A full, read-only root filesystem
- Stale or read-only PID file

/etc/xensource/ptoken

The *ptoken* file is used as a secret, along with SSL, in XenServer pools for additional security in pool member communications.

This topic, along with XenServer's use of SSL, is discussed in Chapter 12.

/etc/xensource/scripts/

The *scripts* directory contains one or more init-level scripts, much like the *master.d* directory.

/etc/xensouce/xapi-ssl.conf

The XenAPI is exposed over port 443, but proper authentication is required to invoke or query the API. In addition to authentication, a certificate private key has to be exchanged to a trusted source to secure further communications to and from a XenServer via SSL-based encryption. This is where *xapi-ssl.conf* is involved because it dictates the cipher, encryption method, and where to store the XenServer's unique certificate.

/etc/xensouce/xapi-ssl.pem

The *xapi-ssl.pem* is a private key that is generated on installation by */etc/init.d/xapissl*, which references *xapi-ssl.conf* to produce a unique Privacy-Enhanced Mail (PEM) file for a XenServer host. This file is what, along with two-factor authentication, is exchanged amongst XenServer hosts, XenServer administration tools, etc., to secure communications back and forth to a unique, specific XenServer host.

Replacing the *xapi-ssl.pem* file with a self-signed or signed certificate is discussed in Chapter 12.

/etc/ntp.conf

In our experience, this is probably the most important of all configuration files that a XenServer administrator has liberty to modify at any time. In part, this is due to the nature of system and clock synchronization for precision. But it's also due to the fact that any virtualization solution must facilitate time synchronization across Guest VMs. The Network Time Protocol configuration file—leveraged by ntpd—should never reference a virtual machine and should always reference a local, physical machine with no more than four entries.

While any virtualization solution will do its best to accommodate time drift, if the bare metal host's clock drifts too far off, this can affect scheduling as well as eventually bring a Guest VM down. It is vital that */etc/ntpd.conf* is set up accordingly, per time zone, so the host can appropriately update Guest VMs and their internal clocks. Additionally, if XenServer hosts are pooled, time drift between hosts must be minimized, and NTP settings be identical on all pool members.

/var/xapi/

This directory contains the complete XAPI database, which is a reference of hardware utilized within a standalone XenServer installation or pool installation.

System State Information

Files within the */var/xapi/* directory contain state information and should never be manually edited under any circumstance. If modified, virtualization performance can become degraded because the XAPI database is based off the collective hardware, objects, and dependencies for virtualizing Guest VMs.

/var/patch/ and /var/patch/applied/

These two directories—*/var/patch/* and */var/patch/applied/*—are extremely important because between the two, they contain the footprint of hotfixes, patches, and other maintenance metadata that is essential for XAPI. Whether you have a standalone XenServer or a pool of XenServers, XAPI has to have a means to ensure that the following sequence has been successfully performed:

1. Patches have been applied to a standalone host.
2. Patches have been applied to all hosts in pool.
3. All post-patch actions, such as a reboot, have been accomplished.

Now, while both directories contain files with unique, UUID-based filenames, it is worth noting that the most important directory is that of */var/patch/applied/*, because as the name implies, this contains a minimal footprint for patches that have been applied to a host.

This directory—*/var/patch/applied/*—should never be deleted because it is used by XAPI to check if a pool member needs a patch applied to it, if there are new hotfixes available for your XenServer host, and so on. As such, deletion of these files could lead to a host incorrectly seeing itself as requiring a patch.

XenServer Object Relationships

While dom0 is in charge of controlling a host's resources, it is also responsible for creating objects that represent portions of host resources. These objects are stacked to ensure that a VM's operating system perceives real hardware, which is in reality a virtual representation of physical hardware. The difference is that these objects are assigned to a specific domU, protected, queued, and handled by dom0 to facilitate the flow of I/O for seamless virtualization. The key hardware types used across all XenServer deployments are network devices and disk storage. If the VM is hosting graphics-intensive applications, the virtualization administrator may need to assign a virtual GPU to it as well.

All objects are assigned universal unique identifiers (UUIDs) along with a secondary UUID that is known as an opaque reference. While physical objects will have a static UUID for the life span of the object, virtual objects can change depending upon system state. For example, the UUID of a virtual device may change when the VM is migrated to a different host. These distinct identifiers aide with mapping of resources to objects, as well as provide the XenServer administrator means to track such resources with xe.

Network Objects

From an architecture perspective, a XenServer deployment will consist of three network types: primary management, storage, and VM traffic. The default network in all XenServer installations will automatically be assigned to the first available network interface and that network interface will become the primary-management network. While all additional network interfaces can be used for storage or VM traffic, and can also be aggregated for redundancy and potentially increased throughput, the primary-management network is key because it is responsible for:

- Allowing administrator access through authenticating tools, such as XenCenter
- Sustaining a communication link amongst pooled XenServer hosts
- Negotiating live VM migrations
- Exposing XAPI to third-party tools

Understanding the relationship between XenServer network objects is critical to properly defining a network topology for a XenServer deployment.

Planning for Multiple Pools

Although we're focused on the design and management of a single XenServer pool in this book, if your requirements dictate multiple pools, you should account for that in your design. This is particularly true for infrastructure that can be shared between pools such as the network and storage systems. Details on these subjects can be found in Chapter 5.

pif

The pif object references the physical network hardware as viewed from within dom0. Because dom0 is CentOS based, the default network will be labeled "eth0" and will be assigned the IP address of the XenServer host. All additional physical networks will be represented as "ethX" but only physical interfaces with a "Management" or "Storage" role will have assigned IP addresses. The list of all physical network interfaces can be obtained from the command line as shown in Example 2-9.

Example 2-9. Which interfaces are configured on a host

```
# xe pif-list params=all
```

network

Because a XenServer will typically host many virtual machines that need to be connected to a network, a virtual switching fabric is created. Each fabric bridges all hosts in a XenServer resource pool and is implemented using the Open Virtual Switch or ovs. The number of virtual switches contained in a XenServer environment will vary and can often be dynamic. The list of all networks can be obtained from the command line as shown in Example 2-10.

Example 2-10. Which networks are configured for a host

```
# xe network-list params=all
```

The logical connection between `network` and `pif` is maintained by the `PIF-uuids` field.

vif

Each VM in a XenServer environment will typically have at least one virtual NIC assigned to it. Those virtual NICs are each called a `vif` and are plugged into the network fabric. All `vifs` are assigned a MAC address by XenServer. Often, network administrators look for virtual NICs to have a MAC vendor ID that they can then filter on. Because XenServer was designed to handle a large number of VMs, the vendor ID of a universally administered MAC address would artificially limit virtual networking so XenServer uses locally administered VMs to avoid the potential of MAC collision.

The IP address a `vif` receives is set by the guest and communicated to XenServer through an interface in the XenServer tools. Because the XenServer network fabric implements a virtual switch, each `vif` plugs into a `network`, which in turn plugs into a `pif` representing a physical NIC that is then connected to a physical switch. The list of all virtual network interfaces can be found using the command line shown in Example 2-11.

Example 2-11. Current virtual network configuration for all VMs in the pool

```
# xe vif-list params=all
```

bond

Optionally, administrators can configure redundant network elements known as "bonds." NIC bonding, also referred to as "teaming," is a method by which two or more NICs are joined to form a logical NIC. More on bonding can be found in "Define Network Topologies" on page 58. The list of all bonded networks can be found using the command line shown in Example 2-12.

Example 2-12. Determine current bond configuration

```
# xe bond-list params=all
```

If a bond is defined, the "master," "slaves," and "primary-slave" configuration items all refer to `pif` objects.

GPU Objects

XenServer supports the use of graphics cards with VMs. A physical graphics card can be directly assigned to a VM; and with certain NVIDIA and Intel chips, the physical card can also be virtualized. This allows the capacity of a single card to be shared through virtual GPUs.

pGPU

A physical graphical processor unit (pGPU) is an object that represents a physical video card, or graphics engine, that is installed as an onboard or PCI device on the physical host. Example 2-13 shows the command to get a list of all pGPUs installed for a host, as well as an example of results after running the command.

One example of a pGPU is an onboard VGA chipset, which is used by dom0 and its console. Example 2-14 shows the command to use to find the default GPU being used by dom0. Unless a dedicated graphic adapter or the host has a CPU with embedded GPU capabilities, the primary pGPU detected on boot is the only one that can be utilized by XenServer. Certain graphic adapters can be used in either GPU pass-through mode where the entire GPU is assigned to a VM, or in virtualized graphics mode where a portion of the GPU is assigned to different VMs.

Example 2-13. Determine physical GPUs installed for a host. Result shows a NVIDIA Quadro present.

```
# xe pgpu-list
uuid ( RO)              : 47d8c17d-3ea0-8a76-c58a-cb1d4300a5ec
        vendor-name ( RO): NVIDIA Corporation
        device-name ( RO): G98 [Quadro NVS 295]
     gpu-group-uuid ( RW): 1ac5d1f6-d581-1b14-55f1-54ef6a1954b4
```

Example 2-14. Determine the default GPU used by dom0

```
# lspci | grep "VGA"
```

gpu-group

A GPU group is simply a collection of graphics engines that are contained within a single, physical graphics card. If the graphics card is able to partition its resources into multiple GPU objects, then a GPU group will contain a reference to each object, as shown in Example 2-15.

Example 2-15. List GPU resources associated with physical graphics adapter

```
# xe gpu-group-list
```

vgpu

A `vgpu` represents a virtual graphics adapter as defined by the graphics card. The `vgpu-type-list` command shown in Example 2-16, returned three possiblevGPU options for the given host.

Example 2-16. View the GPU types within a XenServer host

```
# xe vgpu-type-list
uuid ( RO)              : ad32125b-e5b6-2894-9d16-1809f032c5bb
     vendor-name ( RO): NVIDIA Corporation
      model-name ( RO): GRID K100
framebuffer-size ( RO): 268435456

uuid ( RO)              : ee22b661-4aa0-e6e6-5876-e316c3ea09fe
     vendor-name ( RO): NVIDIA Corporation
      model-name ( RO): GRID K140Q
framebuffer-size ( RO): 1006632960

uuid ( RO)              : 2025cc3e-c869-ef44-2757-a1994cc77c8e
     vendor-name ( RO):
      model-name ( RO): passthrough
framebuffer-size ( RO): 0
```

Storage Objects

From an architecture perspective, storage will consist of two concepts represented by four distinct objects. Each is uniquely identified and maintained within the XAPI database and are as follows:

- Storage repositories (SRs) are physical devices that will contain the virtual disks associated with a VM.
- Physical block devices (PBDs) map physical server storage to a storage repository.
- Virtual disk interfaces (VDIs) are virtual hard drives that leverage a storage-management API: keeping the disk type hidden to the VM, but transactions handled accordingly by the hypervisor.
- Virtual block disks (VBDs) map VDIs to virtual machines.

The relationship between these four objects is shown in Figure 2-4.

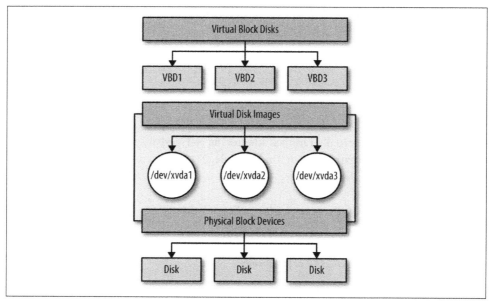

Figure 2-4. How XenServer storage objects relate to one another

## CHAPTER 3

Installing XenServer

The most important design decision you'll need to make is defining the overall purpose for your XenServer installation. Many years ago, Citrix had a marketing campaign called "Ten minutes to Xen." The core premise behind that campaign was that XenServer was so easy to install, a manual install could be completed in less than 10 minutes. This was a particularly interesting premise, considering that alternate platforms could easily take 10 minutes to simply collect configuration information, and it even prompted one analyst to arrive with a stop watch and slow-booting hardware to test the premise; and still the full install completed in less than 10 minutes.

XenServer is a complete operating environment that is installed onto the target host's local storage media. The installer does not support operating environment selection on boot (commonly known as dual-booting), and XenServer should be installed on a dedicated host. While there are frequent requests to install XenServer on removable Flash-based media, doing so should be avoided in order to preserve the lifespan of the media. Likewise for USB-based storage: do not install XenServer onto such media because it has been tested, tried, and presents extreme performance issues.

At the writing of our book, TRIM support is not a part of the kernel. As such, XenServer can be safely installed on solid-state drives (SSDs) whose controllers have the appropriate logic to ensure specific cells aren't prematurely aged. Otherwise, the absence of TRIM or other implementations means it will only be a matter of time before SSD-based installs experience reliability issues as the media slowly becomes read only.

Overview of Key Concepts Only

This chapter covers core concepts you will need to know when installing XenServer. It isn't a replacement for the installation and administration guide found in the documentation set for the version of XenServer you intend to deploy.

Dundee Changes

Preview versions of XenServer Dundee have included updated file layouts and installation options. Because there is no guarantee further modifications won't occur, what is described in this chapter represents XenServer 6.5.

The installer creates a bootable partition for dom0 while utilizing the remaining disk space for local storage. Swap is file-based for performance and is created on boot, mapping to */var/swap/*. Figure 3-1 gives a basic overview of the disk layout after installing XenServer onto a host's local hard drive.

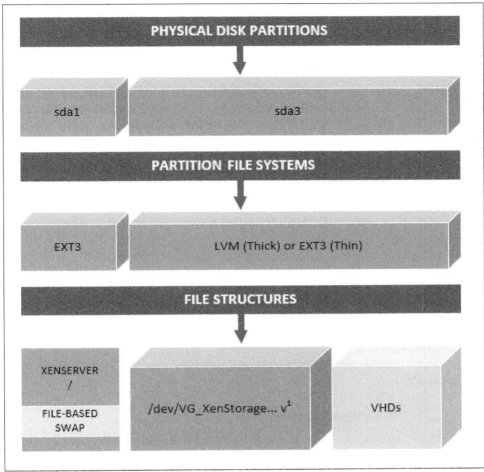

Figure 3-1. File layout post-installation

Manual Installation

In a manual installation, the XenServer installation ISO image is either burned to a bootable CD or copied to a bootable Flash device. The target XenServer host then boots from the installation media and can be installed. Manual installation is typically used when the number of hosts to be deployed is small, and either physical access to the host exists or access to a remote host console such as HP's Integrated Lights Out (iLO) or Dell's Remote Access Console (DRAC).

During a manual installation, the user will be prompted for a variety of information, but the most important configuration items relate to networking.

Please refer to the section "Define Network Topologies" on page 58 for more information.

Unattended Installation

XenServer supports installation using network boot. In this model, a PXE and DHCP server with TFTP service available are used. The installation media is extracted from the source ISO and placed in a FTP, HTTP, or NFS location. The bootloader is extracted from the installation media and placed on the TFTP server.

Boot from SAN

XenServer supports the ability to boot from a remote SAN when either a Fibre Channel or iSCSI HBA with an HBA BIOS enables the XenServer host to locate the boot media on a SAN.

Supplemental Packs

Optional XenServer components are delivered using supplemental packs in ISO format. A supplemental pack can contain any functionality that requires modification of dom0—related to functionality or third-party vendor drivers—that will enable specific functionality to a XenServer host. Because a supplemental pack modifies dom0, it's important to note that older supplemental packs are not supported on newer XenServer installations.

Docker Supplemental Pack

During our work with this book, the XenServer 6.5 SP1 release included a supplemental pack for Docker. This ISO image for Docker-specific functionality can be downloaded from *http://xenserver.org/open-source-virtualization-download.html*.

Third-Party Driver Disks

While a standard XenServer installation contains drivers for a large number of hardware devices, like any operating system driver disks will occasionally be required. Drivers are created using the XenServer Device Driver Kit (DDK) with the full procedure being documented in the XenServer Driver Development Kit Guide for each version of XenServer. The DDK is used by both hardware vendors to create drivers for hardware that wasn't available at the time of shipping and Citrix Support with the help of vendors to address hardware and firmware issues.

If you needed a driver disk to install or recognize your hardware, it's important to understand how driver disks work in a XenServer system and how they impact operational decisions. Drivers are interfaces between the physical hardware and an operating system. In the context of XenServer, they interface with the custom Linux kernel in dom0. Because a given XenServer update might include an updated Linux kernel, if you have used a custom driver, it's important to validate if a kernel update is included.

If a kernel update is part of a given XenServer update, then you will need to further validate if an updated driver exists for this new kernel. It's not uncommon for driver updates to lag behind kernel updates for a number of reasons, so check first to minimize downtime.

## CHAPTER 4

Design Assumptions Impacting Deployment

As interesting as the "Ten minutes to Xen" campaign mentioned in Chapter 3 was, it glossed over the real-world planning that goes into successful deployments. Before starting any deployment, it's vital to define what the goal behind the installation is, what types of workloads it'll have, and what service-level expectations are associated with those workloads. It is far too easy to create either a killer deployment that costs more than it should or a deployment that hosts critical workloads but lacks proper redundancy or capacity.

In this chapter, we'll cover some of the factors that go into "right sizing" a deployment for production use or simply in a test lab.

Pooled Hosts Versus Standalone Hosts

A XenServer pool is a collection of standalone hosts that operate as a single resource: sharing identical hardware, identical setup, and the same shared resources. VMs deployed on one host can be readily migrated to another member host, and the pool master serves as the single point of management. Because the primary purpose of a pool is to provide a single resource made of multiple members, it's important to understand what this means from a VM perspective.

Figure 4-1 provides an example of a typical, standalone XenServer host and its resources. The resources are owned and controlled by this single host: from local storage to any direct-attach storage (DAS).

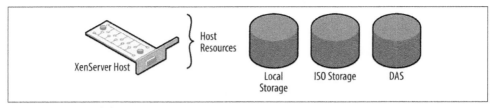

Figure 4-1. Standalone XenServer

In Figure 4-2, we can see an example of multiple hosts—configured as a pool—and that pool resources, such as ISO storage or shared storage allocated for VM disks, can be managed by all hosts within the pool.

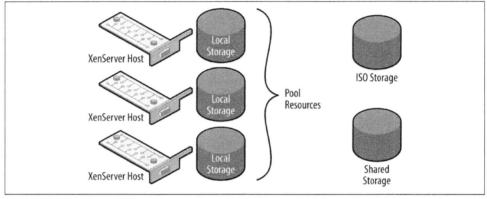

Figure 4-2. Pooled XenServer hosts

Pool Master Versus Pool Member

When XenServer is deployed using a pooled model, the pool master is the primary management point for the pool and its member hosts. Configuration changes should always be first applied to the pool master and then replicated to member servers. This replication ensures that any pool member can become a master if required.

In the event a pool master fails, the remaining member servers will continue to function with known good information, but it can be difficult to make configuration changes. To manually elect a new pool master while the pool master is functional, issue the command in Example 4-1 from the member server you wish to become the new master.

Example 4-1. Designating a new pool master in healthy pool

```
# xe pool-designate-new-master uuid={uuid of new host}
```

If the pool master has failed and become unavailable, and XenServer HA isn't enabled, the commands in Example 4-2 can be used to designate a new pool master.

Example 4-2. Recovery from failed pool master

```
# xe pool-emergency-transition-to-master uuid={uuid of new host}
# xe pool-recover-slaves
```

If XenServer HA is enabled, a replacement pool master will be nominated by the surviving member servers and automatically promoted to pool master. Depending upon your provisioning solution, it may be necessary to reconfigure it to recognize the new pool master.

Processor Compatibility Within Pools

When a VM is started, the virtual CPUs assigned to that VM are allocated from the physical CPUs in the host. Those physical CPUs have an instruction set defined in them, as well as certain processor features that are collectively known programmatically as *physical features*. Modern operating systems are aware of these capabilities, and often, applications rely on specific extensions to perform at their peak. This translates into the VM operating system being very aware of its underlying CPU capabilities. If a resource pool is constructed with hosts having identical processors (CPU type and stepping), then VMs can freely migrate between hosts in a pool without risking stability.

On the other hand, if the processors are different in a pool, instabilities can occur.

For example, if a VM is moved to a host that lacks a CPU instruction the original host had, it's very likely for that VM to crash, or worse, corrupt some data. In XenServer this problem is solved using Intel FlexMigration or AMD Extended Migration, as appropriate. Through the use of this technology, a host with a newer CPU can be added to an existing resource pool, but with the newer CPU downgrading itself to the older features. Not all CPUs can be downgraded to the same point, and it's always possible that no common set of features was defined by the processor vendor. To determine if a new host is compatible with the existing pool members, issue the command in Example 4-3 on both the new host and a member server.

Example 4-3. Determine CPU capabilities

```
# xe host-cpu-info
```

If the physical_features of a new host's CPU are a superset of the existing pool master's CPU physical_features, then it may be possible to add the new host to the existing pool. This concept is referred to as CPU Masking, where the CPU with the lowest set of physical_features becomes representative of the pool. From a technical perspective, masking allows old and new processors of the same architecture, family, and sometimes generation to coexist in a XenServer pooled deployment.

The masking comes into play allowing the lowest common denominator, or lowest processor with the least CPU features, within the pool to not be exposed or aware of the more advanced or newer features present in newer processors.

Forcing a Host into a Pool

While it is possible to force a new host into a pool without regard for feature masks, this process should never be performed in a production environment. Doing so can cause significant stability problems with VM migrations if a VM is migrated to a host with different CPU instructions.

If a pool has long since been established with homogenous hardware, instead of adding newer hosts, it is recommended to build out a second pool based on the new hardware, capacity need, and tied into its own shared storage to avoid masking issues.

For more information regarding supported CPUs within pooled configurations, please visit *http://hcl.xenserver.org/cpus/*.

Resource Pool Sizing

When someone asks about pool sizing, it's always impressive how often the goal is "bigger is better." A XenServer pool consists of a pool master and some number of member servers. The compute collection is then used to host VMs that run some type of workload. For example, how you design a pool to handle XenDesktop workloads is very dependent upon the fact that users will expect a seamless desktop experience from the VMs.

If a resource pool should become unavailable for some reason, it's also possible all the VMs in the pool are also experiencing some form of degraded capability. This degraded capability can extend from loss of pool master and potential management of the pool through to shared resource failure. Using this model, a server should be no bigger than required to host the maximum number of VMs you can tolerate losing in the event of hardware failure. By extension, a pool should contain no more hosts than you are willing to experience degraded operation for.

Maximum Hosts per Pool

Every version of XenServer has included a configuration limit covering how many hosts could reliably be placed in a pool. For some customers, this number has felt insufficient. In reality, there is no hard limit to the number of hosts that can be placed in the pool. Important factors such as the number of VMs running on each host and the number of XAPI operations occurring within the pool have direct impact on the pool size.

Because it is difficult to determine a precise value for each parameter, we instead provide guidance on pool sizes. Occasionally, a given provisioning solution such as XenDesktop might determine that for its needs a smaller maximum pool size is warranted.

When to Create a New Pool

While it is possible to extend a pool with newer hardware, the best practice may instead be to create a new pool with the updated hardware. Masking CPU features is fantastic when you are looking purely at fresh capacity, but the mask will disable capabilities in the new CPU, which may impact performance. If your original XenServer installation is now at a utilization level that demands extra capacity, you should look back at the rationale used to originally define the pool size.

If the pool size was defined around failure tolerance, then adding capacity to an existing pool could represent additional risk. Creating a new pool would allow for the new hardware to perform at its peak and your pool design and associated risk profile to remain valid.

Because a pool is a collection of hosts working to support a common goal, it's important to account for the workloads in the pool when defining a pool. Factors to account for could include:

- Compliance requirements, which dictate how VMs are to be deployed or managed.
- Performance considerations of VMs, which could impact the number of VMs a host is able to support.
- Data sensitivity, which might impact where a host is deployed within an organization. For example, if a XenServer pool is hosting VMs that are public facing, it may not be appropriate for it to also host VMs containing financial information.
- Unique hardware dependencies present within a workload. For example, a GPU-intensive VM will require access to a GPU, but you can only install a limited number of GPUs in a host due to power and cooling contraints.

Defining a Management Paradigm

XenServer has a fantastic distributed architecture, but it is only as efficient as its administrators. When defining a use for a XenServer pool, you will need to define how it will be managed. If management isn't planned in the design phase, it's entirely possible for the resultant architecture to be challenging to operate.

Provisioning Tools

If your XenServer infrastructure is to form part of an Apache CloudStack, OpenStack, or XenDesktop environment, those tools will define how VMs are to be provisioned. Each of these tools will assume they have complete ownership over the XenServer resources, and manual changes could easily break things. Nominally simple tasks such as applying security patches or performing hardware maintenance can be complicated if the provisioning tool expects a consistent configuration.

This problem is easily encountered during planned activities such as patching but can be particularly problematic when emergency activities are necessary. Administrators are strongly encouraged to perform the backup operations listed in Chapter 10, but to also retain configuration information for key items such as pool management interfaces.

Multiple XenCenter Administrators

XenCenter is a graphical management tool that can be installed on any Microsoft Windows machine. Because XenServer has a distributed architecture, it isn't required to have XenCenter constantly running, and many XenServer installations are never managed from within XenCenter. If you do use XenCenter and have multiple XenServer administrators, it's important to understand how XenServer commands work.

XenCenter is fundamentally a graphical user interface (GUI) around the XAPI. As such, it takes login credentials and establishes a session with a given XenServer resource pool. Multiple resource pools can be administered from within a single XenCenter session provided they use the same credentials. Because XenCenter is fully aware of what role a user has within a given XenServer resource pool, it is entirely possible for a user to have different access rights within different pools.

When a user requests an action to be performed (e.g., start a VM), XenCenter maps that command to the corresponding XenAPI call and issues it. Multiple concurrent commands can be executed; and while XenCenter naturally sequences commands based on user input, when multiple users are accessing the same resource pool, oddities can happen.

Consider, for example, the case of starting a VM. The VM power state can only be "HALTED," "RUNNING," "PAUSED," or "SUSPENDED." If you attempt to start a VM that is already running, an error will be returned. This is precisely the type of administrative "oddity" that can occur with multiple administrators attempting to perform the same action. In the event an unexpected error occurs when attempting to perform a task, verify the state of the error in the XenCenter notifications area. It will show which user performed the task and will also include those tasks performed via API and command line.

Hardware Compatibility

Like many operating systems, XenServer has a hardware compatibility list, or HCL. That HCL can be found at *http://hcl.xenserver.org* and lists all the hardware that Citrix and the hardware vendor agree to deliver support for. In effect, the hardware listed represents hardware that is known to work with XenServer and for which the vendor still offers production support.

So if the hardware you wish to use isn't listed, that doesn't mean XenServer won't install and run perfectly fine. What it does mean is that either Citrix hasn't yet tested the hardware, in which case you can submit to have it tested from the HCL website, or that the vendor doesn't wish to support its hardware for the given XenServer version. This is a particularly important consideration for production use and is an important item to verify prior to performing a version upgrade. With legacy hardware that was previously on the HCL, XenServer often will function without issue upon upgrade, but it is important to test first.

Host Requirements

Installation of XenServer can occur on the vast majority of x86 server class hardware available today. The core requirements are to have the server boot from a BIOS (or legacy mode if using UEFI) and enable virtualization extensions for your chosen CPU. While XenServer can be installed onto workstation or desktop class machines, the performance and reliability of those machines are only appropriate for test labs.

Dundee Changes

XenServer Dundee has delivered preview access to a XenServer that can be installed on UEFI-capable machines.

It has been our experience that, XenServer aside, having one or more bare minimum hosts to test internally before rolling out to production is of benefit to production. Certain tests within a lab will never scale to production levels, but the majority of XenServer-related administrative tasks can be carried out within a lab environment to better prepare, plan, and document what should be done going into production changes.

In our test environments, we keep one or more hosts with the following "bare minimum" resources available before rolling out changes to our production-grade environments:

- Multisocket/multicore AMD or Intel-based host
- 8 GB–12 GB of physical RAM
- 100 GB or more of spindle-based storage
- 1 or more gigabit-based networking cards
- Guest VMs that reflect those in a production environment

As for production grade hardware and host requirements, this will be discussed further in Chapter 5.

BIOS, Firmware, and Driver Updates

The HCL contains very specific information regarding various peripherals, drivers, and firmware used during the certification process for XenServer. As such, it is critical that a particular component's firmware (provided by a vendor) matches the HCL. Drivers distributed with the XenServer installation media or in subsequent patches are developed against a given component and firmware level. This is done to ensure the desired functionality as well as for performance with respect to the function of said component.

So, for you administrators, always ensure that your hosts have the latest BIOS, firmware, and additional software from your vendor applied to each host before installation, forming a pool, or upgrading to a newer XenServer version.

Driver Updates and XenServer Updates

If the default installation of XenServer doesn't contain a driver for your hardware, or you installed a hardware driver post XenServer installation, pay particular attention to XenServer updates. A XenServer update may downgrade your driver, and the driver and kernel version requirements in a XenServer update are listed in the release notes.

Shared Versus Local Storage

Local Storage is storage that is a part of the host's hardware, such as spindle or SSD-based drives. After XenServer has been installed onto a host, the remaining disk space is left as local storage. This storage is also managed by the host's native hardware and maintained by dom0. For many on a budget, this is quite sufficient because drive capacity in comparison to price is quite cheap. It also means that all VMs are stored on the same drive or drives and do not require complex storage networks, such as with Fibre Channel, iSCSI, or NFS.

Shared storage is the opposite of local storage in that it facilitates much of what a local disk drive would do, but that other authorized XenServer hosts can also leverage this. It is also important to note that not only can multiple hosts use this storage for virtual-machine disks, snapshots, and configuration data, but provisioning applications and other third-party utilities can leverage this storage via the XAPI API. Shared storage is always remote, such as an iSCSI chassis, Fibre Channel array, or NFS container that leverages standardized storage area network protocols with each XenServer host.

Historically, building a XenServer resource pool using only local storage meant giving up the ability to live migrate a VM between hosts using the XenMotion feature. Xen-Motion of a VM was accomplished in part by transferring ownership of the underlying virtual block device from one XenServer host to another. Because local storage was tied to a given host, such vbd transfer wasn't possible until Storage XenMotion was implemented in XenServer 6.1.

Storage XenMotion allows the disk of a VM to be moved from one storage repository to another, without powering off the VM. The migration can be between different storage implementations and can both occur between local storage and shared storage and across XenServer resource pools. With the flexibility Storage XenMotion provides, the automatic decision to choose shared storage isn't as strong a requirement for certain deployment scenarios such as those supporting cloud operations.

Storage Provisioning Model

Storage is provisioned in XenServer using storage repositories to contain virtual disks. Based on the needs of a XenServer deployment, two different types of storage provisioning are available to meet the needs for a deployment that scales, but is also manageable: thin or thick provisioning. The choice of provisioning model will both dictate certain storage topologies and have a direct bearing on storage consumption.

During the design phase of a XenServer deployment, it is best to decide upon which of the two provisioning methods should be used. The primary reason for this is that, over time with data accumulation, converting a storage device's provisioning method may be time consuming, complex, and in certain cases, impossible based on storage limitations.

Thick provisioning

A thick-provisioned storage device ensures that the allocated size for a storage volume will represent the consumed size regardless of how much of the device is actually used. From the perspective of the XenServer administrator who has just created a Guest VM with a 60 GB virtual disk, the storage device immediately reports its total space, minus 60 GB. While the Guest VM's virtual disk may only use 20 GB of physical space, the thick-provisioned storage device blocks of 60 GB of "used space" despite the 40 GB of "empty space." This is to ensure the virtual disk will always have its 60 GB of potential storage available to the Guest VM as well as preventing the overlap, or over provisioning of the storage device's physical size.

As the storage management APIs talk to the storage device, which is thick provisioned, it considers and reports:

- I have that space available.
- The administrator has permission to create a virtual disk.
- I will pre-allocate 60 GB of disk space for this VM.
- I will subtract 60 GB from my total.
- I will present all of this back to the administrator through XAPI.

Finally, a high-level overview of thick-provisioned, logical-volume managed storage devices is presented in Figure 4-3. It is important to note that if any of the logical volumes (LVMs) are close to full, more space for new virtual disks, snapshots, and backups will not be possible until space is "freed" or "returned" to the storage device as usable space.

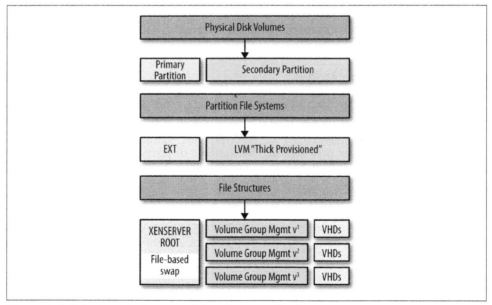

Figure 4-3. Relationship between disk volumes and volume groups

Thick Provisioning Is a Default for iSCSI and HBA

The iSCSI and HBA storage repositories use a thick-provisioned storage model. As discussed earlier, this means the virtual disk consumes its full configured size on the storage solution. While this can be designed for a running VM, it's important to realize that any snapshots are also thick provisioned. Without accounting for this extra storage, its quite easy to run low on storage without clear indication why.

Dundee Changes

XenServer Dundee has provided access to preview functionality that includes support for thin provisioned block storage.

Thin provisioning

In contrast to "thick provisioning," storage that is thinly provisioned will only consume physical storage that compares to its actual usage. In the case of a VM, that is allocated a 60 GB disk but is only consuming 20 GB of that disk, the underlying storage will see roughly 20 GB consumed. This overprovisioning of storage has a clear benefit but also comes with distinct risks.

The most immediate benefit to VM administrators is that expensive storage solutions can be utilized more efficiently. Consider a deployment that will use 80 GB disks for each VM but on average will only have 20 GB used. If the available storage is 5 TB, this means you can comfortably fit roughly 64 VMs on that storage solution when thickly provisioned. Changing to thin provisioning will result in up to 256 VMs being able to fit within that same storage footprint. Considering the cost of storage, this is a definite benefit, but adds the additional management burden of ensuring disks whose usage increases, won't exhaust the available storage of the physical hardware.

NFS Storage Is by Default Thin Provisioned

When using NFS-based storage, it's important to monitor the free space on your NAS to ensure sufficient free space exists to account for VM growth. If monitoring isn't in place, it is quite possible to run out of storage on the underlying storage, particularly if snapshots and disk clones are used.

Sparse allocation

Sparse allocation occurs when the physical disk layout doesn't contain contiguous blocks. For example, if you write a single file at the start of the disk and another at the end of the disk, the middle isn't allocated. When working with thinly provisioned disks, it is very likely the filesystem the VM is using is sparsely allocated. This allows the disk to report low disk utilization because the unused portions of the disk can be represented as empty blocks.

When using thinly provisioned disks, it's important to understand how the filesystem is actually represented on disk and how unused file blocks are handled. Consider the case of a file that gets deleted.

If when a file is deleted, the filesystem simply updates a file table indicating the blocks to be free, then to the underlying storage the blocks freed may still look like they are in use. If the storage is sparsely allocated, and the storage has no way to know the file was deleted, then it will assume the blocks to be in use resulting in increased storage utilization. In this scenario, copying of files within the VM could actually cause disk usage to increase when thinly provisioned. A real-world example of this occurs with disk defragmentation tools and can occur within certain applications that use just-in-time compilation.

Storage I/O Operations Per Second (IOPS)

All storage solutions have a maximum number of I/O operations they can perform per second. Factors governing the maximum IOPS for a storage solution include the size of transfer, the storage controller, the RAID level, and the physical disk characteristics. As a general rule, the faster the physical disk spins, and the more disks in the RAID-set, the more I/O you can generate, with solid state storage having the highest I/O. As with most things in computing, faster means more costly, so it's important to understand if you really need all the speed you think you do.

Validating Local Storage

Historically, XenServer administrators used shared storage to enable live migration of VMs. Starting with XenServer 6.1, shared storage was no longer required to live migrate a VM. This opened the potential for local storage to be used, without losing the benefit of live migration. While there are distinct performance benefits for using shared storage for live migration, if you rarely need to migrate a VM, local storage could benefit you, and at a potentially lower cost.

The key to determining if local storage is sufficient for your needs is to look at the IOPS you require, and the size of the storage. IOPS per disk will vary from well over 5000 for SSD to roughly 125 for SATA 10K. The formula to determine the number of VMs a disk array can handle is:

$$VMs = \frac{disks \times \text{IOPS per disk} \times \left(\text{read percentage} + \frac{\text{write percentage}}{\text{RAID write penalty}}\right)}{\text{IOPS per VM}}$$

Using a single SSD with 5000 IOPS and 30 IOPS per VM, we are able to handle roughly 150 VMs per host, while using eight SATA 10K disks in a RAID 10 configuration with 30% writes would result in 28 VMs on the same host. If each VM requires 40 GB, the SSD solution requires six terabytes of SSD, which can be expensive and will likely require multiple drives making shared storage attractive, while using SATA 10K the requirements can be met with eight drives.

Memory Management

Memory management within a XenServer host can be a bit confusing for some. This confusion only increases when Internet searches reference increasing dom0 memory utilization for certain types of workloads. In this section, we'll cover the basics of memory usage within a XenServer environment, but should you believe it beneficial to increase dom0 memory, you should do so only under the guidance of support services.

Fixed Memory Concepts

Fixed memory represents a memory object that is fixed within the system. Examples of fixed memory include the physical memory in a host, the memory consumed by the hypervisor, and memory used by dom0.

Host memory

Host memory is the physical memory present within a XenServer host. While it is possible to overcommit host memory, at no point in time can there be running VMs whose allocated memory exceeds the physical memory contained within a host. Determining the host memory via command line is shown in Example 4-4.

Physical Hot Plug or RAM

XenServer currently doesn't support hot plug of host memory. If the physical memory configuration needs to be changed, place the host in maintenance mode, evacuate all VMs to other hosts, and perform the hardware reconfiguration.

Example 4-4. Determine current host memory configuration

```
# xe host-list uuid=[host-uuid] params=memory-total,memory-free
```

Hypervisor memory

Hypervisor memory is used by the core Xen hypervisor, the crash kernel, and core tooling. It is referred to as the "host memory overhead," and is obtained using the memory-overhead parameter, as shown in Example 4-5.

Example 4-5. Determine hypervisor memory overhead

```
# xe host-list uuid=[host-uuid] params=memory-overhead
```

dom0 memory

dom0 memory is used by the control domain. Because the control domain is a specialized virtual machine, correct configuration of its memory is important to optimum performance. Each XenServer version has had recommendations on the maximum memory configuration for dom0, and with XenServer versions 6.2 and prior, many of the recommendations were a balance between Linux low-memory requirements and user space. Starting with XenServer 6.5, dom0 became 64 bit, and with that change, all previous best practices with respect to memory configuration should be avoided. dom0 memory will be automatically sized based on the physical memory configuration but may need to be resized based on specific hardware devices (drivers that need more memory) or specific usage scenarios (adjustment for cache utilization).

It's strongly recommended that such changes be performed with the guidance of support services. Example 4-6 shows you how to obtain the current memory utilization in dom0. It starts with determining the UUID of the control domain or dom0.

Example 4-6. Determine current memory utilization within dom0

```
# xe vm-list is-control-domain=true
# xe vm-list uuid={dom0-uuid} \
params=memory-actual,memory-overhead
```

The total memory used will be the sum of `memory-actual` and `memory-overhead` expressed in bytes.

> **dom0 Memory and Performance**
>
> If you suspect a performance problem within dom0 that might be related to memory usage, the Linux `top` command can help. Using `top`, look for swap memory used. If the value is high, then dom0 is under memory pressure and a higher value might be warranted.

Dynamic VM Memory Management

Dynamic memory management, also known as dynamic memory control, is a mechanism within XenServer that allows the configured maximum memory of all running VMs to exceed the physical memory within a given XenServer host. This allows for efficient utilization of host memory while maximizing VM density. It is important to note that when host memory is overcommitted, VM performance can suffer, and that recovery from host failures is made more complex. As a result, extreme utilization of dynamic memory should be avoided where possible.

Implementation

Dynamic memory management is implemented within dom0 using the `squeezed` daemon and within the Guest VM using the XenServer tools with an operating system memory balloon driver. This balloon driver is configured with the maximum and minimum dynamic memory settings. When the VM starts up, XenServer configures the VM with the maximum memory. This allows the operating system to define any memory access tables and caches appropriately. The operating system then loads its drivers, which then causes the XenServer balloon driver to be loaded. The balloon driver then reserves as much free memory as possible to either provide the operating system with available memory equal to the dynamic minimum memory, or some value of memory between minimum and maximum. If the host has sufficient free memory for the VM to use its configured maximum, the balloon driver releases all memory back to the operating system.

In the event a VM requests to load on a host, XAPI will call `squeezed` to process the memory-allocation request. If there is insufficient free host memory, `squeezed` sends a request into all running VMs on the host requesting they free any unused memory. The balloon driver in each VM responds by attempting to reclaim any free memory it had reserved at startup and reports the result back to `squeezed`. If after the process of memory reclamation completes there is sufficient memory to load the VM, then normal VM start occurs. If there wasn't sufficient memory, an insufficient memory error is returned via XAPI to the caller.

Enabling dynamic memory management

Dynamic memory management is automatically enabled for any VM that is running the XenServer tools, and for which the dynamic memory parameters are configured. The dynamic memory parameters are `memory-dynamic-max` and `memory-dynamic-min`, and they are closely related to their static memory cousins, `memory-static-max` and `memory-static-min`. XenServer enforces the following memory relationship for dynamic memory within a VM:

`memory-static-min` ≤ `memory-dynamic-min` ≤ `memory-dynamic-max` ≤ `memory-static-max`

It's important to note that with each supported operating system, the XenServer engineering team explicitly tests the limits of dynamic memory for that operating system. This can result in different bounds for memory configuration than what the vendor or operating system author provides. Often this discrepancy is due to observed instabilities in the operating system at the lower bound for dynamic memory. If no observed instabilities are present, then the minimum value for dynamic memory will be defined at the pool level as one quarter of the static maximum for the operating system.

Changing the memory configuration on a VM is easily performed from within Xen-Center, which will automatically validate the configuration and any restart requirements. In example Example 4-7, we see the command line method for changing the minimum value for dynamic memory on a specific VM. Example 4-8 shows how to verify the running configuration for a given VM.

Example 4-7. Change dynamic memory using CLI

```
# xe vm-param-set uuid=[vm-uuid] memory-dynamic-min=2147483648
```

If Dynamic Memory Constraints Are Violated

Error code: MEMORY_CONSTRAINT_VIOLATION

Error parameters: memory limits must satisfy: static_min $\leq$ dynamic_min $\leq$ dynamic_max $\leq$ static_max

Example 4-8. Determine current memory configuration

```
# xe vm-list uuid=[vm-uuid]  params=all
```

Migration of VMs to other hosts

When a VM is migrated to another host, it's possible the new host lacks sufficient memory to run the VM. In order to attempt migration, XAPI first requests via squeezed that the VM being migrated reduce its memory requirements as much as possible. This then establishes a minimum running configuration whose values are then communicated via XAPI to the XAPI daemon on the destination host. XAPI on the destination host takes the memory requirements and communicates them to squeezed as if the migrating VM were starting. Assuming the VM can start, migration will proceed. In the event migration can't proceed, an insufficient memory error will be returned via XAPI to the caller.

Planning for Infrastructure Failure

Modern data-center operations assume some level of infrastructure failure will eventually occur. XenServer provides a number of options intended to provide resiliency in the face of failure. Examples include bonding and link aggregation of networks and multiple paths to storage; both of which are covered in Chapter 5. In addition to resiliency, XenServer can be configured to self monitor for host failures and automatically restart impacted virtual machines.

Host Failure Protection

Host failure protection, or high availability (HA), uses a combination of network and shared storage heartbeat monitors to determine if a given host within a resource pool is operating. In the event the requisite heartbeat interval isn't satisfied, the Xen hypervisor watchdog will trip and self-fence the host. This has the direct benefit of ensuring that crashes and instabilities from within dom0 are also trapped. In the event the pool master is deemed to have failed, one of the surviving hosts—in a discussion with the remaining hosts—will promote a suitable host with enough resources as the new pool master. The pool master then automatically restarts any VMs configured to restart in the event of host failure that were running on the failed server, and VM operations continue with minimal interruption.

Host failure protection isn't designed to detect a VM that crashes or operate with a pool with fewer than three hosts and does require that all protected VMs have no affinities to a specific host and have their disks on shared storage. If host failure protection is required for resource pools with fewer than three hosts, an external monitoring and attestation service will be required. The creation of such a service is beyond the scope of this book.

Host failure protection also requires that each member within a XenServer pool has multiple paths to both storage, management infrastructure, and other essential networks. In regards to network, this is accomplished via bonded networking; and for iSCSI and Fibre Channel storage, this is accomplished with multipathed storage networks. Even without the host-failure protection enabled, multipathed storage and bonding can help eliminate single points of failure within the storage, management, and infrastructure network.

Protection levels

VMs in a pool can be protected as "best effort," "protected," and "unprotected." Within each category, a restart priority can be given. Any VM with protected status will automatically be restarted in priority order if there is sufficient remaining capacity to do so. The XenServer pool master continually monitors the status of member servers, and if insufficient capacity existed to restart all protected and best-effort VMs, as new capacity becomes available, the pool master will automatically restart any remaining protected and "best effort" VMs.

XenServer HA can be enabled by issuing the command in Example 4-9, where `heartbeat-sr-uuids` is the UUID of the shared storage repository on which the heartbeat metadata will be written.

Example 4-10 shows the command for disabling XenServer HA.

Example 4-9. Enable XenServer HA

```
# xe pool-ha-enable heartbeat-sr-uuids={SR-UUID}
```

Example 4-10. Disable XenServer HA

```
# xe pool-ha-disable
```

Configuration of which VMs to protect is easily done using XenCenter but can also be performed from the command line. Example 4-11 shows how a specific VM can be configured to automatically restart as the first VM in the restart order. Note that the order parameter is optional.

Example 4-11. Specifying a VM to automatically restart

```
# xe vm-param-set uuid={vm-uuid} ha-restart-priority=restart \
order=1
```

Preventing Aggressive Fencing

Occasionally XenServer will determine that a storage heartbeat failure has occurred and fence a host, or worse, an entire pool. This typically occurs when a redundant storage solution or a storage solution with redundant controllers is used, and the failover timer used by the storage solution is longer than the default XenServer HA timeout of 30 seconds. The value for this timeout can be changed, but it's important to know that simply enabling HA from within XenCenter, or using the default form of the pool-enable-ha command will reset the timeout to the default value.

In Example 4-12, the timeout has been increased from the default to two minutes.

Example 4-12. Set HA timeout to prevent aggressive fencing

```
# xe pool-enable-ha heartbeat-sr-uuids={SR-UUID} \
ha-config:timeout=120
```

Capacity Planning During Failure

Ensuring sufficient capacity to restart protected hosts is a key result of the HA plan created by the HA daemon. This plan takes into account the current operational state of every protected VM, and also the state of each host. If dynamic memory control is enabled, available free host memory, current VM memory consumed per VM, and minimum required memory for protected VMs is factored into the plan.

As you can imagine, the more hosts in a pool and the greater the number of protected VMs, the more complex the HA plan becomes. To account for these complexities, the

XenServer HA daemon computes the maximum number of host failures that can be tolerated and still allow for all protected VMs to run.

To determine the current maximum failure count, issue the command in Example 4-13.

Example 4-13. Determine the current maximum host failures that can be accepted

```
# xe pool-ha-compute-max-host-failures-to-tolerate
```

If the failure count is three or fewer, the HA daemon will compute a failure plan that accounts for most eventualities and can accommodate hosts with dissimilar configurations. If the host count is greater than three, the HA daemon assumes that every VM is as large as the largest, and that every host is as densely populated as the most densely populated host. As a result, for most production deployments, it will be important to set the maximum host failures to as few as required to meet the operational requirements for the pool.

To set the maximum number of host failures, issue the command in Example 4-14.

Example 4-14. Set the maximum host failures to accept

```
# xe pool-param-set ha-host-failures-to-tolerate={count}
```

No Single Points of Failure

To a certain extent, this should be obvious, but you'd be surprised at how often complaints are raised against XenServer that are really the result of single points of failure in the deployment. Under normal operation, XenServer configuration information is automatically replicated between all member servers in a pool, and the final arbiter of sanity is the pool master. This means that any member server can become a pool master as needed with minimal interruption of XenServer operations. Replication of configuration information always occurs over the primary management network, which implies the primary management network should have redundant links. Similarly, if shared storage is used, it is assumed the VMs will be updating some information on their attached virtual disks, so redundant network connections are also required for storage networks. It is of course not sufficient to simply have multiple NICs in the host and bond them together; network redundancy must also exist within the network switches between hosts and to storage.

## CHAPTER 5

Deployment Blueprint

In this chapter, we'll cover some of the decision points you'll want to go through in order to optimize the design of your XenServer deployment. While it might be tempting to call these "best practices," it would be more accurate to describe them as a simple decision tree. The core topics covered are storage and networking as they relate to creating a stable deployment with predictable performance.

Start with Storage

All VMs will need their disks to be stored someplace, and it's important in your blueprint to decide how the VM interacts with the resources you provide. In Chapter 4, we covered pools versus standalone hosts, shared versus local storage, defining an input/output (I/O) envelope, and designing for failure.

Each of these items has storage at its core, so in the following sections, we'll provide a basic decision matrix.

Local Versus Shared Storage

If you use local storage in a resource pool, all I/O associated with those VMs is local to the host. This can be beneficial if the VMs have compatible I/O requirements. One of the drawbacks to local storage is that VM migration will be more resource intensive, slower, and have a greater user impact than with shared storage due to the usage of storage migration. During storage migration, the underlying disk is copied from the source storage to destination storage, and this copy occurs over a management network. Because the primary management network is used for all pool operations, the copy operation can also impose a performance penalty on VM provisioning and pool maintenance.

Another form of VM agility that is impacted by local storage is XenServer HA, or host failure protection. Because XenServer HA requires heartbeat storage and an agile VM, the use of local storage will prevent a VM from being restarted in the event of host failure.

NFS Versus iSCSI

Within the storage community, there has been a long debate over which is more efficient, Network File System (NFS) or Internet Small Computer System Interface (iSCSI). In this book, we're not going to enter that debate, but it is important to understand how XenServer uses storage with each of these technologies. The first, and arguably most important, item to understand is that from a XenServer perspective, NFS is always thinly provisioned, while iSCSI is always thick provisioned. This means that if you have a VM with a 20 GB disk with 12GB used, on NFS you will only use 12 GB while on iSCSI you will always consume 20 GB.

This point becomes even more important as you include the concept of snapshots because they, too, will be provisioned with the underlying storage. In other words, if we have our original VM and then take a snapshot that results in an additional 1 GB of disk used, on NFS, we'll only be using 13 GB, while on iSCSI, we'll have 40 GB consumed. Factoring in snapshot usage can have a significant impact on the choice of storage interface, but it's not the only one.

Dundee Changes

XenServer Dundee has provided early access to functionality that includes the option to create thin-provisioned block storage.

Fibre Channel and HBAs

Fibre Channel (FC) describes both the technology and protocol (based on SCSI) for high-speed storage. As the name indicates, the technology utilizes host bus adapter (HBA) cards that utilize fibre connections: connecting to a specialized switch or directly into the controller for the storage. From a XenServer perspective, storage operations involving HBAs will be very similar to those of iSCSI-based storage. The primary difference is in the connection and transport, and where we describe iSCSI operations, limitations, and best practices, those same attributes can be applied to Fibre Channel or HBA-based storage.

Converged Network Adapters

When we sat down to write this book, converged network adapters (CNAs) were quite popular because they allow optimized storage traffic to traverse over Ethernet. With XenServer 6.5, few CNAs are officially supported; and in many cases where used, it is generally the Ethernet capabilities that can be leveraged. Of note, hardware FCoE support was added in XenServer 6.5 service pack 1 with a limited set of hardware vendors. As an administrator, make certain to cross reference fibre-based storage solutions with the XenServer hardware compatibility list for compatibility.

Multipath Configurations

In production deployments, having minimal single points of failure is desired. If NFS is used as the storage solution, this is accomplished by bonding multiple storage network interface controllers (NICs) to form a redundant link to the NFS server. More on bonding can be found in the section "Define Network Topologies" on page 58. While it is possible to use network bonds with iSCSI, a far more common scenario is to use multiple physical network paths to multiple storage controllers. Such a configuration ensures that multiple independent interfaces to the storage can be maintained. Figure 5-1 shows how a single session established from a host to a storage target operates. In this scenario, network failure would result in loss of session and by extension loss of the underlying storage for all VMs using the storage target. By contrast, Figure 5-2 shows that loss of a single session in a multipath configuration will result in failover to remaining sessions.

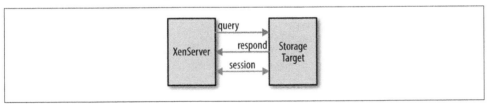

Figure 5-1. Without multipathing: single session, single point of failure

From a blueprint perspective, it's important to understand how each path is maintained within XenServer. As a refresher, for block storage, a storage repository (SR) is the logical unit number (LUN) on which the VM disks will be stored. There is a physical block device (PBD) interface between the SR and the storage manager.

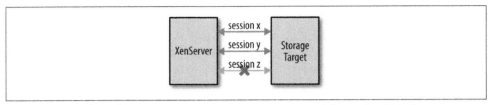

Figure 5-2. Multipathing: sessions X & Y sustain storage while session Z is down

This means that for each path in a multipath configuration, there will be one PBD to plug into the storage manager. Because the length of time required to plug a given interface in is a function of storage controller response time, having a large number of LUNs per host in a multipath configuration can result in extended host restart times. This presents a natural trade-off between potential increased system redundancy, input/output per second (IOPS) per controller, IOPS per LUN, and host recovery time.

Because the goal of a multipath configuration is redundancy, proper design requires redundant physical infrastructure. This can include backplanes, switches, fabric extenders, and will often include tuning the storage per vendor best practices.

All trade-offs, tuning decisions, and redundancy assumptions should be defined at the design phase and documented. In Example 5-1, we see that procedure to enable multipath storage on a host, and the reader should note that this operation requires the host to be disabled, which will evacuate or stop all running VMs.

Example 5-1. Enabling multipath configurations on XenServer

```
# xe host-disable host=[hostname]
# xe host-param-set other-config:multipathing=true
    \ host=[host uuid]
# xe host-param-set other-config:multipathhandle=dmp
    \ uuid=[host uuid]
# xe host-enable host=[hostname]
```

Define Network Topologies

Within a XenServer environment, there are several potential network topologies, but all require that hosts within a resource pool have identical configurations. An identical configuration will be one with the following attributes:

- Consistent enumeration of NICs across reboots. If the host BIOS changes the device order for NICs between two reboots, this can cause significant issues to XenServer.
- Consistent network interfaces between hosts. This is best explained with an example. Regardless of which physical NIC the BIOS assigns to "eth0" in a given

host, "eth0" for all hosts identifies a management network that will utilize the same switch. The same requirement must be met for all interfaces, and a consistent interface is one which is identical in all parameters including frame rate and size.

- Framing must be consistent within a network interface. This is also best explained with an example. If the frame size for "eth2" is Jumbo, then all host network interfaces within the "eth2" network must be set to "Jumbo."
- Network speed must be consistent within a network interface. It is not possible to mix 1 Gb and 10 Gb NICs within the same network, and the same extends to duplex settings.
- All networks with assigned IPs (management interfaces) must be within the same broadcast domain. While it may be possible to have management traffic span network segments, doing so could result in inconsistent state between member servers in a pool, and not all management functions are guaranteed to function.
- All networks with assigned IPs must have single-digit latency or better.
- When Virtual LAN Segments (VLANs) are used for management interfaces, the network switch port must be configured to provide a default VLAN that is configured as "not-tagged" by the switch.

Bonding and LACP

NIC bonding, also referred to as "teaming," is a method by which two or more NICs are joined to form a logical NIC. Bonded NICs provide a redundant connection and in certain configurations can increase aggregate throughput. XenServer supports three distinct bonding modes: `active-backup`, `balance-slb`, and Link Aggregation Control Protocol (LACP).

active-backup bonding

With an `active-backup` bond, one interface in the bond is designated as active, and all other interfaces are backups. In the event the link is lost for the active interface, a backup with a link will be selected to replace it. Figure 5-3 shows a bonded network with eth0 and eth1 forming the bond where eth1 is the backup. No traffic flows over eth1 until the connection to eth0 fails, at which point the bond automatically operates, as shown in Figure 5-4.

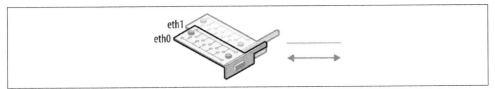

Figure 5-3. eth0 active, with eth1 ready as a backup

With an `active-backup` bond, it is assumed that redundant network paths exist so when a backup is selected the network will use Gratuitous Address Resolution Protocol (GARP) for all interfaces; including any VMs on the network.

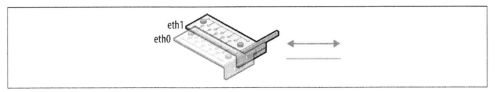

Figure 5-4. eth1 active, taking over responsibilities for ETH0

This bonding mode is supported for both Linux bridge and Open vSwitch (*http://openvswitch.org/*) based bonds and assumes stacked switches (Example 5-2).

Example 5-2. Create active-backup bond

```
# xe bond-create mode=active-backup network-uuid=<network-uuid> \
  pif-uuids=<pif-uuids>
```

balance-slb bonding

With `balance-slb` bonding, a source-load-balancing active bond is created with balanced traffic. This means that all interfaces in the bond are used, with traffic balanced between the interfaces based on load and source VM MAC address. Balancing based on source media access control (MAC) address implies that transmit and receive traffic for a given VM will always occur over the same path. Example 5-3 shows the command to create a `balance-slb` bond.

The traffic flow is rebalanced every 10 seconds by default, but this can be defined when the bond is created. When traffic is rebalanced, the physical route to a given VM through the network bond may change. `balance-slb` uses the standard Linux `balance-alb` algorithm at its core, which requires the network driver support dynamic rewrite of the MAC address in order to avoid Address Resolution Protocol (ARP)/GARP during rebalancing. This bonding mode is supported for both Linux bridge and Open Virtual Switch based bonds and assumes stacked switches. Note that if network monitoring is done at the physical interface layer, data can be lost during a balancing event.

Example 5-3. Create balance-slb bond

```
# xe bond-create mode=balance-slb network-uuid=<network-uuid> \
  pif-uuids=<pif-uuids>
```

LACP bonds

LACP bonds are created to support link aggregation or 802.3ad (802.1AX-2008, as defined by the IEEE at *http://www.ieee802.org/3/ad/*). LACP is only supported by the Open Virtual Switch and requires physical switches configured for LACP using LACP data units (LACPDU). Cisco EtherChannel and Port Aggregation Protocol (PAgP) are not supported. LACP can be configured for up to four interfaces per bond. LACP determines traffic flow by default based on a hash of the source and destination IP, TCP/UDP port, and source MAC address. Example 5-4 shows the command to create a LACP bond.

Due to the increased parameters in the hash when compared to `balance-slb`, LACP bonds can result in transmit and receive traffic to a given VM following different paths. Because destination IP and port are used in the hash, LACP bonds may provide limited throughput gains when traffic is occurring to a single destination.

An example of such a configuration would be use of LACP for storage traffic where the storage solution is an NFS server, or an iSCSI controller with a single path. In both configurations, the hash will compute to bind traffic to a single member NIC within the bond, which will result in LACP behaving as an `active-backup` bond.

Example 5-4. Create LACP bond

```
# xe bond-create mode=lacp network-uuid=<network-uuid> \
  pif-uuids=<pif-uuids>
```

Jumbo Frames

Jumbo frames are Ethernet frames that carry more than 1,500 bytes of payload, or more than the standard maximum transmission unit (MTU). While no standards exist to define jumbo frames, storage and hardware vendors offer end-to-end support for Ethernet frames, which can carry up to 9,000 bytes of payload. It's important to understand that with a lack of standard, the precise MTU value for a given network device can vary by vendor. Ensuring compatible MTU values is crucial to realizing the performance benefits jumbo frames can offer to storage traffic. If the MTU in any device in the data path is smaller than either the source or destination device, packet fragmentation will result, and the resultant retransmissions will impact overall throughput.

XenServer defines a jumbo frame using a MTU of 9,000, and jumbo frames are only supported for use on storage networks. Example 5-5 shows the command line operations to perform in order to ensure the MTU is correct on all elements of the physical interface.

Example 5-5. Verify MTU on all networks

```
# xe pif-list params=uuid,network-name-label,MTU
# xe network-list params=uuid,name-label,MTU
```

## CHAPTER 6

Understanding Guest VM Types

While XenServer supports many different operating systems, there are two types of Guest VM virtualization modes: hardware virtual machine (HVM) and para-virtualized (PV). While a third, PVHVM, will be briefly discussed, the primary distinction between these is related to the Guest VM's operating system.

HVM Guests

HVM requires specialized extensions present in modern Intel and AMD processors. These extensions are known as Intel VT-x or AMD-V and allow the physical CPU to trap certain CPU instruction sets that operating systems normally use to interact with a bare metal server. Were an operating system to execute those instructions when virtualized, other VMs might be impacted.

HVM is commonly used when virtualizing an operating system such as Microsoft Windows where it isn't possible to modify the operating system in order to make it virtualization aware. Because HVM guests have no awareness of their virtualization, they typically use emulated device drivers. In order to improve the performance of hardware-sensitive operations like disk or network access, HVM guests are usually installed with the XenServer tools. These tools provide operating system-specific drivers that are optimized for use in a XenServer environment and provide significant performance increase over an emulated driver.

PV Guests

Unlike HVM guests, para-virtualized guest VMs are aware they are virtualized and load an optimized kernel for the target hypervisor. Linux is a perfect example of an operating system that can be para-virtualized. While mainstream Linux distributions are generally Xen aware, certain distributions may require admins to recompile the kernel in order to enable Xen awareness. Historically, it was viewed that para-virtualization was the optimal solution for Linux guest VMs, but the most recent Linux releases include a kernel that is Xen aware and that operates in a cooperative manner with Xen, allowing these guests to perform best in HVM mode.

Microsoft Windows in XenServer

One can install and immediately virtualize a Windows Guest without PV drivers, also known as the XenServer Tools. The issue is that without the PV drivers, XenServer is providing emulated devices for the Windows Guest VM. Without the PV drivers, performance bottlenecks are quickly reached, particularly when some Windows VMs are used to run SQL Servers (Structured Query Language), Active Directory, and other infrastructure services. Additionally, the performance impact of emulation will lead to performance and scalability degradation in the XenServer host.

The XenServer tools provide optimized drivers for Windows network, storage, and video virtual hardware. These three components are key to running a high-performance Windows infrastructure, and as such, it is important that the XenServer tools used in a Windows VM match those for the XenServer host. Using older tools can lead to degraded performance and in certain circumstances degraded stability.

HVM versus Linux PV

As mentioned earlier, recent changes to Linux mean that Guest VMs perform optimally in HVM mode. Examples of these newer Linux distributions include CentOS 7, RHEL 7, Ubuntu 14.04, Debian Jessie, and SLES 12.

Looking to the Future with PVHVM

As the Xen hypervisor and XenServer continue to evolve, one of the most exciting features is that of PVHVM, or running Linux with HVM extensions. Overall, this is the most efficient form of virtualization and can be seen with Ubuntu, Debian, CentOS, and many popular releases with Xen-ready kernels. Still acting as a PV guest VM, PVHVM can leverage HVM extensions so that video and other aspects of the modern Linux experience can be leveraged.

## PART II

Management Recipes

While being able to design a XenServer deployment is the ideal way to create a XenServer environment that follows best practices, that's not always an option and is only part of being a successful XenServer administrator. Whether you have inherited an existing deployment, perhaps with minimal design notes, or you are facing daily management tasks, we're going to cover some common management actions in this section.

Such tasks range from the simple act of installing a XenServer to potential panic situations like being locked out of a host or needing to conduct hardware maintenance. We're calling this section "management recipes" because we really want to empower you with successful procedures. The format will present a specific problem, describe a solution, and either discuss the rationale behind the solution or provide steps to implement it. In all situations, we'll be giving only what's required because if you're like us, when something needs fixing, it needs fixing now.

## CHAPTER 7

Installation Recipes

Installation of XenServer can be accomplished in minutes using a variety of methods. Selecting the correct method will depend in part on the scale of your intended deployment and your hardware configuration. In addition to covering installation of XenServer, this chapter also covers driver management and the installation of extra components via supplemental packages.

Manual Installation

Problem

Installation of XenServer is desired to either perform a proof-of-concept or creation of a small XenServer pool.

Solution

Download the installation media from *http://xenserver.org/download*, and either burn it to a CD/DVD or create a bootable USB Flash device.

Discussion

In a manual installation, the XenServer installation ISO is either burned to a bootable CD or copied to a bootable Flash device. The target XenServer host then boots from the installation media and can be installed. Manual installation is typically used when the number of hosts to be deployed is small, and either physical access to the host exists or access to a remote host console such as HP iLO or the Dell Remote Access Console. During a manual installation, the user will be prompted for a variety of information, but the most important configuration items relate to networking. Please refer to the section "Define Network Topologies" on page 58 in Chapter 5 for more information.

Creating a Bootable USB Device

Problem

The ISO that Citrix ships for the XenServer installation media uses an ISO 9660 filesystem appropriate for use with a CD burner, but your server lacks a CD or DVD drive.

Solution

Create a bootable USB key that contains the XenServer installer.

Discussion

Because bootable USB devices make use of the legacy FAT32 filesystem, the ISO shipped by Citrix and available from citrix.com (*https://www.citrix.com/*) and xenserver.org must be converted from ISO 9660 to FAT32. The easiest tool to use for this task is Rufus. Rufus is freely available for multiple platforms and is open source. It is able to create the FAT filesystem, master boot record, and install a version of SYSLINUX, which can then be used to start the standard XenServer installer. No deep knowledge or experience with SYSLINUX is required, nor is there a requirement for a Windows or DOS bootable disk.

Follow these steps to make a bootable USB drive:

1. Download the installation ISO from *http://xenserver.org/download*.
2. Obtain Rufus from *https://rufus.akeo.ie/*.
3. Insert a USB key into your computer with at least 1 GB capacity. Note that installation of the XenServer installer will reformat the drive and delete all data.
4. Create a bootable disk using the ISO option.

In Case the USB Drive Doesn't Boot Right

Note that Rufus defaults for cluster size and legacy BIOS alignment should be correct for most USB keys and fairly modern computers. If the USB key fails to boot correctly, decrease the cluster size to 2048 and select the advanced formatting option for legacy BIOSes. It may also be required to perform a full format of the USB stick to be successful.

XenServer Dundee

XenServer Dundee has an updated ISO installer that has been shown to copy correctly. For Linux users, this means that a simple dd is sufficient to copy the ISO to a USB Flash device.

Unattended Installation

Problem

Installation of XenServer is desired where the installation is performed via PXE boot.

Solution

XenServer supports installation via network boot. Obtain the installation media from *http://xenserver.org/download* and follow the instructions in the following discussion.

Discussion

XenServer supports installation using network boot. In this model, a PXE or DHCP server with TFTP service available is used. The installation media is extracted from the source ISO and placed in an FTP, HTTP, or NFS location.

Validate on One Server First!

This discussion assumes you've already installed XenServer on one server and validated that no additional drivers are required. It also assumes that you've configured you server BIOS to be identical across all servers, and that PXE is supported on the NIC used as the management network. One key item in the preparation is that the servers are set to boot in legacy BIOS mode and not UEFI.

First, you'll need to collect some information by doing the following:

1. Obtain the XenServer installation ISO media.
2. Extract the entire contents of XenServer installation ISO file to either a HTTP, FTP, or NFS location (in this procedure, we'll be using NFS).
3. Collect the information shown in Example 7-1:

Example 7-1. Required configuration parameters

```
Hostname: xenserver
Root password: password
Keyboard locale: us
NTP server address: 0.us.pool.ntp.org
DNS server address: dns.local
Time zone:  America/New_York
Location of extracted ISO file: nfsserver:/
TFTP server IP address: pxehost
```

Configure the TFTP server to supply XenServer installer by following these steps. Example 7-2 contains a script that can be used to perform these steps; simply modify the XenServer ISO extract location to be where you extracted the XenServer files.

1. In the */tftpboot* directory, create a new directory called *xenserver*.
2. Copy the *mboot.c32* and *pxelinux.0* files from the */boot/pxelinux* directory of the XenServer ISO file to the */tftpboot* directory.
3. Copy the *install.img* file from the root directory of the XenServer ISO file to the */tftpboot/xenserver* directory.
4. Copy the *vmlinuz* and *zen.gz* files from the */boot* directory of the XenServer ISO file to the */tftpboot/xenserver* directory.
5. In the */tftpboot* directory, create a new directory called *pxelinux.cfg*.

Example 7-2. Configuration script for tftp server

```
mkdir /mnt/xsinstall
mount [XenServer ISO Extract Location] /mnt/xsinstall
cd ./tftpboot
mkdir xenserver
cp /mnt/xsinstall/boot/pxelinux/mboot.c32 ./
cp /mnt/xsinstall/boot/pxelinux/pxelinux.0 ./
cp /mnt/xsinstall/install.img ./xenserver
cp /mnt/xsinstall/boot/vmlinuz ./xenserver
cp /mnt/xsinstall/boot/zen.gz./xenserver
```

1. In the */tftpboot/pxelinux.cfg* directory, create a new configuration file called *default*.

2. Edit the *default* file to contain the information shown in Example 7-3. Note that this command includes remote logging to a SYSLOG server.

Example 7-3. Example default file

```
default xenserver-auto
label xenserver-auto
        kernel mboot.c32
        append xenserver/xen.gz dom0_max_vcpus=1-2 \
        dom0_mem=752M,max:752M com1=115200,8n1 \
        console=com1,vga --- xenserver/vmlinuz \
        xencons=hvc console=hvc0 console=tty0 \
        answerfile=http://[pxehost]/answerfile.xml \
        remotelog=[SYSLOG] install --- xenserver/install.img
```

Unattended installation of XenServer requires an answer file. Place the answer file in the root directory of your NFS server (Example 7-4). Please note that there are many more options than are listed here, but the information shown in Example 7-3 will suffice for most installations.

Example 7-4. XenServer answer file

```
<?xml version="1.0"?>
<installation mode="fresh" srtype="lvm">
  <bootloader>extlinux</bootloader>
  <primary-disk gueststorage="yes">sda</primary-disk>
  <keymap>[keyboardmap]</keymap>
  <hostname>[hostname]</hostname>
  <root-password>[password]</root-password>
  <source type="nfs">[XenServer ISO Extract Location]</source>
  <admin-interface name="eth0" proto="dhcp"/>
  <name-server>dns.local</name-server>
  <timezone>[Time zone]</timezone>
  <time-config-method>ntp</time-config-method>
  <ntp-server>[NTP Server Address]</ntp-server>
  <script stage="filesystem-populated" type="nfs">
     [XenServer ISO Extract Location]/post-install-script.sh
  </script>
</installation>
```

Boot from SAN

Problem

The server you wish to use for XenServer lacks any physical disk.

Solution

XenServer supports the ability to boot from a remote SAN when either a Fibre Channel or iSCSI HBA with an HBA BIOS enables the XenServer host to locate the boot media on a SAN. The following instructions assume a multipath installation is desired.

Dundee Changes

XenServer Dundee has provided preview functionality of an FCoE based boot from SAN option with additional installer options.

Discussion

Manual installation

When performing a manual installation at the setup prompt, press "F2" and then enter "multipath" as the boot option.

PXE installation

When performing a PXE-based install, the PXE configuration file will need to be modified to support `device_mapper_multipath`, as shown in Example 7-5.

Example 7-5. Modified PXE configuration file to support multipath

```
default xenserver-auto label xenserver-auto
    kernel mboot.c32
    append xenserver/xen.gz dom0_max_vcpus=1-2 \
    dom0_mem=752M,max:752M com1=115200, \
    install --- xenserver/install.img
```

Installation of Supplemental Packs

Some XenServer features are released as supplemental packs. A supplemental pack will contain an installer and is delivered as an ISO.

Problem

A desired feature from a supplemental pack needs to be installed.

Solution

Obtain the supplemental pack and either copy it to dom0, or place it into an ISO storage repository.

Discussion

Optional XenServer components are delivered using "supplemental packs" in ISO format. A supplemental pack can contain any functionality that requires modification of dom0. Because a supplemental pack modifies dom0, it's important to note that older supplemental packs are not supported on newer XenServer installations. Additionally, installed supplemental packs are likely to be disabled during version upgrades to ensure stable operation. In some instances, the contents of a supplemental pack have been directly incorporated into dom0, while in others, core architecture changes render the supplemental pack invalid. The latter is often the case with management agents from third parties until the third party issues a replacement supplemental pack. Installation of a supplemental pack can be done during installation but is more commonly done using the XenServer command line. Examples 7-6 and 7-7 show two different ways of installing a supplemental pack.

Example 7-6. Installation of supplemental pack from local ISO

```
$ xe-install-supplemental-pack {path to ISO}
```

Example 7-7. Installation of supplemental pack from ISO library

```
$ xe-install-supplemental-pack /var/run/sr-mount/{ISO library}/{ISO}
```

Driver Disks

While a standard XenServer installation contains drivers for a large number of hardware devices, like any operating system driver disks will occasionally be required. Drivers are created using the XenServer Device Driver Kit (DDK) with the full procedure being documented in the XenServer Driver Development Kit Guide for each version of XenServer. The DDK is used by hardware vendors to create drivers for hardware that wasn't available at the time of shipping and by Citrix support with the help of vendors to address hardware and firmware issues.

Problem

Driver disks can be required for hardware at boot time but can also be required to address performance issues in a live system.

Solution

Work with the device vendor and Citrix to obtain the correct driver for your hardware. Note that third-party driver disk development often lags behind the release of a new version of XenServer, so it's important to verify driver availability prior to upgrading. In other words, don't rely on a vendor proactively including previously developed drivers in updated XenServer releases.

Discussion

If you needed a driver disk to install or recognize your hardware, it's important to understand how driver disks work in a XenServer system and how they impact operational decisions. Drivers are interfaces between the physical hardware and an operating system. In the context of XenServer, they interface with the custom Linux kernel in dom0. Because a given XenServer update might include an updated Linux kernel, if you have used a custom driver, it's important to validate if a kernel update is included. If a kernel update is part of a given XenServer update, then you will need to further validate if an updated driver exists for this new kernel. It's not uncommon for driver updates to lag behind kernel updates for a number of reasons, so check first to minimize downtime.

Manual installation

When installing XenServer manually, the installer will prompt for driver disks. At this prompt, press F9 on the keyboard and insert the driver media. The installer will automatically load the driver and continue.

Unattended installation

When installing XenServer using an answer file, driver disks can be required to access the network and thus the answer file. In such situations, you will need to modify the XenServer installation media to include the desired driver.

If the driver isn't required to access the answer file, the driver location can be included in the answer file using the `driver-source` with a type of either `nfs` or `url`, as shown in Example 7-8.

Example 7-8. Specifying driver disk source in answer file

```
<driver-source "url">ftp://[ip-address]/[driver]/</driver-source>
```

Resolving driver conflict

Occasionally, XenServer will have a default driver that is incorrectly loaded for a given hardware and prevents the driver disk contents from being used. If the installation is unattended, the driver disk contents should be added to the installer using the process described in the recipe "Slipstreaming Drivers and Supplemental Packs" on page 75. If the installation is manual, you can resolve the driver conflict using this procedure:

1. At the installation boot prompt, type **shell**.

2. At the command prompt, type **rmmod [driver]** where [driver] is the name of the driver in conflict. If no error occurs, the driver has been unloaded and the conflict resolved.
3. Type **exit** and then supply the driver disk manually as outlined previously.

Updating driver post-installation

Because a driver disk is really a special case of a supplemental pack, the easiest way to install a driver disk on a running system is to treat it as supplemental pack, as shown in Examples 7-9 and 7-10.

Example 7-9. Installation of driver from local ISO

```
$ xe-install-supplemental-pack {path to driver ISO}
```

Example 7-10. Installation of driver from ISO library

```
$ xe-install-supplemental-pack /var/run/sr-mount/{ISO library}/{driver ISO}
```

Slipstreaming Drivers and Supplemental Packs

Problem

Your installation requires either third-party drivers or additional features that are delivered on supplemental packs. The goal is to ensure that all XenServer hosts have a consistent installation.

Solution

In order to ensure that all required drivers or supplemental packs are present during the installation, the installation media can be extended to include the additional items.

Discussion

As mentioned previously, XenServer is extended via both driver disks and supplemental packs, both of which are delivered in supplemental pack form. Any supplemental pack can be slipstreamed into the installation media without requiring the installer itself to be modified. The following procedure will create installation media with slipstreamed features:

1. Download the installation ISO for the version of XenServer you wish to deploy.
2. Download the driver disks and/or supplemental packs you wish include.
3. Open the ISO with your favorite ISO editor.

4. Create a single directory for each item to be added. For example, a network device driver might be placed into a directory named *device.NIC*. If more than one item is to be added, each item must be in a unique directory.

5. Into each directory, place the contents of the driver disk or supplemental pack you wish to include.

6. In the root directory of the ISO, edit the *XS-REPOSITORY-LIST* file and include the directories you created in step 4 after the existing items. Only one directory is permitted on a line, and every line must be newline terminated.

7. Re-create the ISO in bootable format.

At this point, you will now have a XenServer installer that includes your slip-streamed features. Installation will proceed with the core XenServer binaries, and all additional features will be installed afterward.

## CHAPTER 8

Planning for Upgrades

The XenServer release cycle consists of a major release, various hotfixes, and optionally at least one service pack. A major release is one where the installation media is generated and doesn't require a major version number to change. After the release, hotfixes are often generated for issues discovered in the wild and to address any security issues discovered.

Depending upon the release cycle, one or more service packs can be created. A service pack will usually contain all previous hotfixes for that version and may also contain new functionality. When a service pack is created, there will be a stated period under which hotfixes will be created for both the major release and the service pack. Once that stated period expires, hotfixes will only be generated for the service pack.

Regardless of whether the upgrade is due to a major release, hotfix, or service pack, the upgrade will include detailed documentation and installation media. It is important as a XenServer administrator to understand where to obtain these updates and how to apply them.

HCL and Upgrades

If you are upgrading to a new XenServer version, please read the section "Upgrades, Support, and Hardware" on page 113 in Chapter 13. At each XenServer version, Citrix updates its HCL in partnership with the hardware vendors. Performing an upgrade in advance of the HCL indicating hardware compatibility could impact your eligibility for support from Citrix and your hardware vendor.

Security Patches

While attaining maximum uptime for virtual infrastructure is a desirable goal, operating a secure environment is arguably more important.

Problem

A security vulnerability has been disclosed by Citrix for XenServer, or a security vulnerability is suspected in XenServer.

Solution

Security disclosures are made by the Citrix Security Response team on the Citrix support site as any new vulnerabilities are discovered. You can receive alerts from the support site by registering at *http://support.citrix.com/profile/watches* and following the instructions there. You will need to create an account if you don't have one, but the account is completely free. Whenever a security hotfix is released, there will be an accompanying security advisory in the form of a CTX knowledgebase article for it, and those same KB articles will be linked on xenserver.org in the download page at *http://xenserver.org/download*.

Discussion

XenServer security patches are almost always prefaced, by Citrix, with a security advisory. The purpose is to inform the community of zero-day threats or known vulnerabilities, such as those in recent years with the attention-grabbing names of Heartbleed, Venom, and Shellshock. Whether a security hole stems from partner projects or XenServer's own code, the security advisories are followed up (as quickly as possible) with a standalone fix for the internal or third-party software affected. Above all, these patches should be applied as soon as possible.

Citrix fully supports responsible reporting of any potential vulnerability. To learn more about how to disclose a potential issue, and for more information on the current security response process, please review the "Reporting security issues to Citrix" (*http://support.citrix.com/article/CTX081743*) page at citrix.com.

Learning of a New Hotfix or Patch

Citrix engineering routinely release updates to XenServer. Keeping abreast of these updates is an important part of operating a healthy XenServer environment.

Problem

You wish to learn about available patches as quickly as possible to plan their deployment.

Solution

Subscribe to Citrix support alerts to learn when a new hotfix is released for XenServer. Users of XenCenter will also automatically learn when an update is available for their specific version via XenCenter notification.

Discussion

You can receive alerts from the support site by registering at *http://support.citrix.com/ profile/watches* and following the instructions there. You will need to create an account if you don't have one, but the account is completely free. Whenever a hotfix is released, a Citrix knowledgebase article will be created for it, and that article will contain instructions for how to obtain the hotfix.

Determine if a Hotfix Is Present

When managing a large installation, or for compliance reasons, it may be necessary to obtain a list of installed XenServer patches.

Problem

Periodic audits of patch status are an important part of compliance.

Solution

Obtain a list of patches applied on each XenServer host.

Discussion

Knowing the current patch status for virtual infrastructure is an important part of securely running XenServer at optimal performance and stability. As part of that process, you should both create a configuration database that lists the expected patch status for a host, and subsequently validate that status. The validation component is readily done with a simple xe command, shown in Example 8-1.

Example 8-1. List all patches on a XenServer host

```
# xe patch-list params=name-label
```

Applying Patches to XenServer

Arguably, the most important step in keeping XenServer hosts healthy is patching, and while the XenCenter management tooling provides a ready method to apply patches, many organizations do not run XenCenter.

Problem

A XenCenter rolling pool upgrade can not be performed either due to lack of Xen-Center usage in a deployment, or a need to script the update.

Solution

A XenServer host can be patched using either the command line or XenCenter. If using XenCenter to patch a XenServer pool, a rolling pool upgrade will be performed. When a rolling pool upgrade is performed, the objective is to patch the pool without incurring VM downtime. To accomplish that task, XenCenter performs a variety of sanity checks and assuming they pass, the pool is upgraded. Details on that process can be found within the XenCenter documentation. In this example, we'll look at how to patch without using a rolling pool upgrade using the the XenServer command line to remotely update a XenServer host.

> ### Dundee Changes
>
> XenServer Dundee has provided preview access to XenCenter functionality that simplifies patch management. While the procedures outlined in this recipe remain valid, XenCenter may provide a more efficient process for future versions.

Discussion

The first step in applying a patch is to download it to a filesystem that the XenServer host has access to. That could be the local filesystem of dom0 or an NFS mount that is mounted in dom0. The patch is then uploaded into XenServer:

```
# xe patch-upload file-name=[local location of PATCH]
```

If the command doesn't return a UUID, then the patch was previously uploaded but not applied. To obtain the required UUID, you'll need to find the patch:

```
# xe patch-list name-label=[Patch name] --minimal
```

With the UUID, the patch can now be applied and its source and temporary files cleaned up:

```
# xe patch-apply uuid=[patch uuid] host-uuid=[host uuid]
# xe patch-clean uuid=[patch uuid]
```

To determine if the patch requires any post-processing, list its guidance:

```
# xe patch-list name-label=[patch uuid] params=after-apply-guidance
```

 Reboots May Be Required

All patches include post-patch guidance, which can include restarting XAPI, restarting HVM or PV guests, or rebooting the entire host. It's important to apply that guidance. The guidance can be found in the hotfix description in the KB article, and also within the patch itself.

## CHAPTER 9

Log Management

Because dom0 is Linux-based, traditional Syslog is used to record information about the kernel, user space processes, virtualization process, as well as user access. With the root partition of a XenServer installation being 4 GB in size, it is important to trend data stored into */var/log/* to prevent a full filesystem. This can be accomplished by tuning */etc/logrotate.conf* or even using Syslog's `forward` method, where logs are sent to a separate host with the job of recording other hosts Syslog-based data.

Syslog is not only a daemon, but also a protocol: it was established long ago for Unix systems to record system and application information to local disk as well as offering the ability to forward the same log information to its peers for redundancy, concentration, and to conserve disk space on highly active systems.

Amusing Digression

For more detailed information regarding Syslog—as both a protocol and daemon—you can review the IETF's specification at *http://tools.ietf.org/html/rfc5424*.

Log Configuration

XenServer provides very detailed operational information in log format. Correct configuration of logs is crucial to ensuring an important event isn't missed.

Problem

As an administrator, you wish to determine which log file will contain what type of information.

Solution

All Syslog configuration information is contained within */etc/syslog.conf*. This file should never be directly edited. From the configuration information, you can determine where each core process places its log information.

Discussion

On a standalone XenServer, the Syslog daemon is started on boot and its configuration file for handling source, severity, types of logs, and where to store them are defined in */etc/syslog.conf*. It is highly recommended that you do not alter this file unless absolutely necessary. From boot to reboot, information is stored in various files found under the root disk's */var/log/* directory.

Taken from a fresh installation of XenServer, Figure 9-1 shows various log files that store information specific to a purpose. Note that the items in brown type are subdirectories.

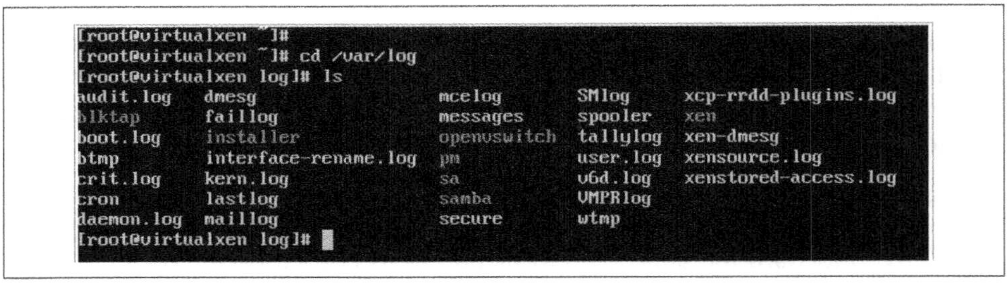

Figure 9-1. Contents of /var/log on a XenServer host

For those seasoned in administering XenServer, the listing shows that from the kernel-level and user-space level, there are not many logfiles. However, XenServer is verbose about logging for a very simple reason: collection, analysis, and troubleshooting if an issue should arise. On a standalone XenServer, logs are received by the Syslog daemon and based on */etc/syslog.conf*—as well as the source and type of message—stored on the local root filesystem as illustrated in Figure 9-2.

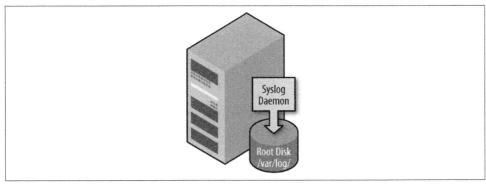

Figure 9-2. Local Syslog daemon interface

Within a pooled XenServer environment, the process is quite similar. Because a pool has a master server, log data for the storage manager (as a quick example) is trickled up to the master server (see Figure 9-3). This is to ensure that while each pool member is recording log data specific to itself, the master server has the aggregate log data needed to promote troubleshooting of the entire pool from one point.

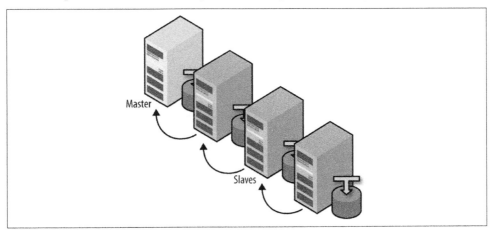

Figure 9-3. Aggregated Syslog for a XenServer pool

Log Rotation

Log rotation governs how frequently the immediate log file is archived, and optionally, compressed. Log rotation also determines how many archived log files to retain prior to old archives being deleted.

Problem

Because the control domain has a fairly small disk size, you are experiencing low disk space issues.

Solution

While some might be tempted to find ways to increase the size of the disk allocated to dom0, doing so presents problems upon upgrade. The better solution is to look at the log usage and rotate logs more aggressively.

Discussion

Log rotation, or `logrotate`, is what ensures that Syslog files in */var/log/* do not grow out of hand. Much like Syslog, `logrotate` utilizes a configuration file to dictate how often, at what size, and if compression should be used when archiving a particular Syslog file. The term "archive" is truly meant for rotating out a current log in place of a fresh, current log to take its place. The older log is then compressed so it occupies less space.

Post XenServer installation and before usage, you can measure the amount of free root disk space by executing the command in Example 9-1.

Example 9-1. Determine free disk space

```
# df -h

Filesystem            Size  Used Avail Use% Mounted on
/dev/sda1             4.0G  1.9G  2.0G  49% /
none                  381M   16K  381M   1% /dev/shm
/opt/xensource/packages/iso/XenCenter.iso
                       52M   52M     0 100% /var/xen/xc-install
```

You can see by the example that only 49% of the root disk on this XenServer host has been used. Repeating this process as implementation ramps up, an administrator should be able to measure how best to tune `logrotate`'s configuration file because, after install, */etc/logrotate.conf* should resemble Example 9-2.

Example 9-2. Default logrotate configuration file

```
# see "man logrotate" for details
# rotate log files weekly
weekly
# keep 4 weeks worth of backlogs
rotate 4
# create new (empty) log files after rotating old ones
create
```

```
# uncomment this if you want your log files compressed
#compress
# RPM packages drop log rotation information into this directory
include /etc/logrotate.d
# no packages own wtmp -- we'll rotate them here
/var/log/wtmp {
    monthly
    minsize 1M
    create 0664 root utmp
    rotate 1
}
/var/log/btmp {
    missingok
    monthly
    minsize 1M
    create 0600 root utmp
    rotate 1
}
# system-specific logs may be also be configured here.
```

Before covering the basic premise and purpose of this configuration file, you can see this exact configuration file explained in more detail at *http://www.techrepublic.com/article/manage-linux-log-files-with-logrotate/*.

The options declared in the default configuration are conditions that, when met, rotate logs accordingly:

1. The first option specifies when to invoke log rotation. By default, this is set to "weekly" and may need to be adjusted for "daily." This will only swap log files out for new ones and will not delete log files.

2. The second option specifies how long to keep archived/rotate log files on the disk. The default is to remove archived/rotated log files after a week. This will delete log files that meet this age.

3. The third option specifies what to do after rotating a log file out. The default—which should not be changed—is to create a new/fresh log after rotating out its older counterpart.

4. The fourth option—which is commented out—specifies how to handle archived log files. It is highly recommended to remove the comment mark so that archived log files are compressed, saving on disk space.

5. A fifth option, which is not present in the default conf, is the "size" option. This specifies how to handle logs that reach a certain size, such as "size 15M." This option should be employed, especially if an administrator has SNMP logs that grow exponentially or notices that the particular XenServer's Syslog files are growing faster than logrotate can rotate and dispose of archived files.

6. The "include" option specifies a subdirectory wherein unique, logrotate configurations can be specified for individual log files.

7. The remaining portion should be left as is.

An example of a daily rotation—set to retain seven days' worth of data with a size limit—shown in Example 9-3.

Example 9-3. logrotate configured to retain seven days of data

```
# see "man logrotate" for details
# rotate log files DAILY
daily

# keep 7 days worth of backlogs
rotate 7

# create new (empty) log files after rotating old ones
create

# uncomment this if you want your log files compressed
compress

# Set a size limit for active logs to prevent large, active logs
size 20M

# RPM packages drop log rotation information into this directory
include /etc/logrotate.d

# no packages own wtmp -- we'll rotate them here
/var/log/wtmp {
    monthly
    minsize 1M
    create 0664 root utmp
    rotate 1
}
/var/log/btmp {
    missingok
    monthly
    minsize 1M
    create 0600 root utmp
    rotate 1
}
# system-specific logs may be also be configured here.
```

Log Aggregation

Single host log management requires access to each host in the environment. With log aggregation, all log information can be centrally accessed.

Problem

Centralized log management and analysis are required for all servers in the data center.

Solution

XenServer fully supports the use of a centralized log server or remote Syslog service.

Discussion

Syslog forwarding is a long-standing feature and one I have been looking forward to explaining, highlighting, and providing examples of. As discussed, Syslog can forward messages to other hosts. Furthermore, it can forward Syslog messages to other hosts without writing a copy of the log to local disk. What this means is that a single XenServer, or a pool of XenServers, can send their log data to a "Syslog Aggregator."

The trade-off is that you cannot generate a server status report via XenCenter, but instead can gather the logs from the Syslog aggregate server and manually submit them for review. That being said, you can ensure that low root disk space is not nearly as high of a concern on the "Admin Todo List" and can retain vast amounts of log data for a deployment of any size; based on dictated industry practices or for, sarcastically, nostalgic purposes.

The principles with Syslog and *logrotate.conf* will apply to the Syslog Aggregator because what good is a Syslog server if not configured properly to ensure it does not fill itself up? The requirements to instantiate a Syslog aggregation server, configure the forwarding of Syslog messages, and so forth are quite simple:

1. Port 514 must be opened on the network.
2. The Syslog aggregation server must be reachable—either by being on the same network segment or not—by each XenServer host.
3. The Syslog aggregation server can be a virtual or physical machine; Windows or Linux-based with either a native Syslog daemon configured to receive external host messages or using a Windows-based Syslog solution offering the same "listening" capabilities.
4. The Syslog aggregation server must have a static IP assigned to it.
5. The Syslog aggregation server should be monitored and tuned just as if it were Syslog/logrotate on a XenServer.
6. For support purposes, logs should be easily copied/compressed from the Syslog aggregation server—such as using WinSCP, scp, or other tools to copy log data for support's analysis.

The quickest means to establish a simple virtual or physical Syslog aggregation server —in our opinion—is to reference the following two links. These describe the installation of a base Debian-based system with specific intent to leverage Rsyslog for the recording of remote Syslog messages sent to it over UDP port 514 from one's Xen-Servers:

http://www.aboutdebian.com/syslog.htm

http://www.howtoforge.com/centralized-rsyslog-server-monitoring

Alternatively, the following is an all-in-one guide (using Debian) with Syslog-NG:

http://www.bbert.com/blog/2010/04/syslog-server-installation-configuration-debian/

Once the aggregation server is configured and ready to record remote Syslog messages, it is time to configure XenServer. This task is easily performed from XenCenter. To begin, click either a pool master or standalone XenServer and from the General tab, select the Properties button:

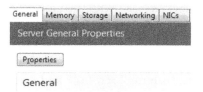

In the window that appears, select the "Log destination" option:

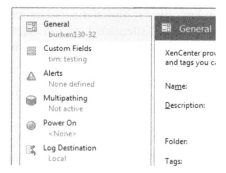

If local logging is configured, the "local" option will be set. Select the "Remote" option and enter the IP address or fully qualified domain name (FQDN) of the remote Syslog aggregate server:

By default XenServer stores its system logs locally on the server. If you wish however you may specify a remote log destination using the settings below.

- ⊙ Local
- ○ Remote
  - Server: [_____]

Finally, select "OK," and the standalone XenServer (or pool) will update its Syslog configuration, or more specifically, */var/lib/syslog.conf*. The reason for this is so Elastic Syslog can take over the normal duties of Syslog: forwarding messages to the Syslog aggregator accordingly.

Certain logs will still continue to record Syslog on the host, so it may be desirable to edit */var/lib/syslog.conf* and add comments to lines where a "-/var/log/some_file-name" is specified, as the lines with "@x.x.x.x" direct the syslog daemon to forward records to the Syslog aggregator. Example 9-4 shows the commands to forward the logs.

Example 9-4. Configure /var/lib/syslog.conf to forward all logs to another host

```
# Save boot messages also to boot.log
local7.*            @10.0.0.1
# local7.*          /var/log/boot.log

# Xapi rbac audit log echoes to Syslog local6
local6.*            @10.0.0.1
# local6.*          -/var/log/audit.log

# Xapi, xenopsd echo to Syslog local5
local5.*            @10.0.0.1
# local5.*          -/var/log/xensource.log
```

After deciding what logs to keep and what logs to forward, Elastic Syslog can be restarted so the changes take effect by executing the command in Example 9-5.

Example 9-5. Restarting Syslog to forward all logs

```
# /etc/init.d/syslog restart
```

Because Elastic Syslog is being utilized, the init script will ensure that Elastic Syslog is bounced and that it is responsible for handling Syslog forwarding, etc.

Throttling SNMP ACKs

Problem

When using the Simple Network Monitor Protocol (SNMP), SNMP acknowledgments (ACKs) are generated filling log files.

Solution

Because most of the SNMP ACKs are for internal operations, they can be safely ignored.

Discussion

If SNMP is being used for monitoring purposes, it is possible that local SNMPD ACK messages can be generated at such a high rate. This puts a burden on Syslog and only uses up more of XenServer's root partition's available space. To ignore these internal acknowledgments, edit */etc/sysconfig/snmpd.options* shown in Example 9-6.

Example 9-6. Edit snmpd.options

```
vi /etc/sysconfig/snmpd.options
# snmpd command line options
# OPTIONS="-Lsd -Lf /dev/null -p /var/run/snmpd.pid -a"
```

At the end of the */etc/sysconfig/snmpd.options* file, append the line in Example 9-7 (leaving the rest intact):

Example 9-7. Append SNMP options

```
OPTIONS="-LS 4 d -p /var/run/snmpd.pid -a"
```

Then restart SNMP:

```
# service snmpd restart
```

## CHAPTER 10

Backup Strategies

The objective of any backup strategy is first to ensure nothing is lost, and second to verify that it can be restored. The reality is that, while this is achievable, with virtualization, we need two distinct paradigms to make this a reality. As we discussed in our design session, a XenServer host has a privileged VM that looks and feels like Linux but has been completely customized. While applying standard Linux backup strategies to it isn't a bad idea, they only go part of the way to supporting the "ensure nothing is lost" criterion. This section will cover those missing pieces.

We'll also touch on what it means to backup a guest VM. While XenServer provides the ability to perform snapshots on running VMs, there are many third-party solutions to manage those snapshots. Unfortunately, many users have discovered that simply having a backup of VMs in snapshot form isn't sufficient. This is because a VM disk by itself lacks the metadata to define the network, memory, and CPU configuration. As a result, any successful strategy needs to encompass both infrastructure and VM backup.

Frequency of Backup

If you are running a XenServer environment that is actively creating and re-creating VMs, then you should pay particular attention to the metadata topics and create an updated metadata backup after each object is configured. In the event a restore is needed and the configuration is stale, errors will be flagged and additional work will be required to restore the pool configuration.

Backup dom0

dom0 is a critical component of all XenServer deployments and should be backed up.

Problem

You wish to back up the core configuration for a single XenServer host, even if pooled.

Solution

XenServer provides a simple command to perform a host backup. This backup should be performed after install and after any reconfiguration or upgrade.

Discussion

In order to back up the core configuration for a XenServer host, a single xe command is used (Example 10-1).

Example 10-1. Backup host

```
# xe host-backup file-name=[filename] -h [hostname] \
  -u root -pw [password]
```

The resultant backup file can then be saved for future use. Note that this is how host-level configuration data is preserved during upgrades, which means that this backup can then be restored onto any fresh installation to re-create the host.

To restore the backup, issue the command in Example 10-2, then reboot using the installation media, and select the "restore from backup" option to complete the restoration.

Example 10-2. Restore host backup

```
# xe host-restore file-name=[filename] -h [hostname] \
  -u root -pw [password]
```

XAPI Database Still Needs to Be Backed Up!

Performing a host backup doesn't back up the XAPI database because it's possible the host is a pool member. To complete a single host backup, you will need to also back up the XAPI database.

Pool and XAPI Database Backup

The XAPI database contains all information related to the XenServer toolstack.

Problem

You wish to back up the XAPI database and associated pool configuration.

Solution

XenServer provides a simple command to perform a backup of the XAPI database. This backup should be performed after install and after any reconfiguration or upgrade.

Discussion

The XAPI database contains all information related to the current pool configuration. This includes storage, network, VM, GPU, user, and host information. Having a current backup of the pool metadata will greatly simplify the process of restoring a pool after a major hardware issue, such as a storage controller failure. To create a backup of the pool metadata, issue the command in Example 10-3.

Example 10-3. Backup pool metadata to NFS mount

```
# xe pool-dump-database file-name=[NFS backup]
```

In the event the metadata needs to be restored, issue the command in Example 10-4 on the host.

Example 10-4. Restore pool metadata

```
# xe pool-database-restore file-name=[backup file]
```

Performing a Dry Run

The pool-database-restore command has an optional parameter called dry-run. If set to "true," the command will verify the integrity of the backup and issue any warnings that might prevent a successful backup.

VM Backup

Guest virtual machines come in essentially two configurations: stateless VM or stateful VM. Stateless VMs have no meaningful state information in them and often lack a backup model. Instead, the provisioning solution simply re-creates them as required.

On the other hand, a stateful VM contains some material information, be it configuration information or data. Stateful VMs are often part of a backup strategy.

Problem

You wish to back up an individual VM and its configuration without downtime.

Solution

While XenServer supports a VM export command that will perform a full backup of a VM, this command requires the VM be powered down. In order to perform a snapshot of a running VM, you will need to take a snapshot of that VM, export any VM metadata, and then export the snapshot.

Discussion

Creating a VM backup in a crash-consistent manner is easily accomplished using snapshots. Crash-consistent VMs are ones that automatically recover from a hard shutdown, which could occur from a power outage.

1. Start by locating the VM's UUID, which will be used throughout this procedure:

   ```
   # xe vm-list name-label=[VM name] --minimal
   ```

2. Then create a snapshot for the VM, which also returns a UUID:

   ```
   # xe vm-snapshot uuid=[uuid] new-name-label=[snapshot name]
   ```

3. Next convert the snapshot into a VM:

   ```
   # xe template-param-set is-a-template=false uuid=[snapshot uuid]
   ```

4. Then export the VM with all associated metadata:

   ```
   # xe vm-export vm=[snapshot uuid]filename=filename.xva
   ```

5. Then clean up by removing the snapshot and requesting storage garbage collection to be run:

   ```
   # xe vm-uninstall uuid=[snapshot uuid] force=true
   # xe sr-scan uuid=[SR uuid]
   ```

The exported VM can then be restored onto any XenServer host with a compatible XenServer version to the original host.

Account for Snapshot Chains

When using snapshots as a part of a backup strategy, it's important to understand disk chains. Snapshots collected by virtual appliance-based or external solutions can pose a risk to successful backups. The primary reason is that, after 28–30 snapshots, a mathematical limitation of VHD files with excessive snapshots is encountered. Even with a base disk still intact, it becomes difficult, time-consuming, and storage intensive to coalesce those snapshots back into a base VM disk. Furthermore, if the base disk is lost, there is no alpha point with which to base snapshots off of to revert to a previous moment in time of a Guest VM's life.

Metadata Backup and Restore

Throughout this book, we have placed heavy emphasis in avoiding single points of failure and disaster recovery. In considering both of these major topics for a single-server or pool-configured deployment, this section discusses how to back up and restore VM metadata in the event of a host failure.

As each VM is created, information is stored within XAPI's database. This information, known as metadata, describes each VM, its physical resource requirements, and its virtual resources requirements. This data includes, but is not limited to:

- VM name and description
- Boot order and OS information
- Virtual network information
- Virtual disk definitions and locations

In the event of a complete host or pool failure, there are scenarios where recovery of VMs can be an arduous task or worse, impossible to restore without metadata backups.

Problem

You wish to back up all relationships between a virtual machine and the virtual infrastructure.

Solution

Virtual machine metadata can be backed up onto shared storage. When combined with backups of other information, including the VM disks, this ensures that a full recovery of a XenServer environment can occur.

Discussion

Metadata backups can be created at will in xsconsole, XenCenter, or from the command line within dom0. While we will focus on the command line, the end result from either source is a backup of all current VM metadata stored in a virtual disk (VDI) container. The reason for this format is so that, like a VM's VDI, it can be moved, exported, or accessed by pool members.

Avoid Single Points of Failure

Metadata backups should always be stored on a shared storage repository. Local storage should never be used because this backup now becomes a single point of failure in the event of disk corruption.

The xe-backup-metadata utility can be executed manually—or automated—from the command line. Example 10-5 shows you the command to obtain all backup options, while Example 10-6 shows the command to back up to a specified SR.

Example 10-5. Obtain all backup options

```
# xe-backup-metadata -h
```

Example 10-6. Back up metadata to specified SR

```
# xe-backup-metadata -c -i -u [SR UUID for backup]
```

Restoring metadata requires that the XenServer host be operational and that the SR on which the backup is present has been added. Once those requirements have been met, the metadata back up can be restored, as shown in Example 10-7.

Example 10-7. Restore all metadata on the specified SR

```
# xe-restore-metadata -u [UUID of Shared Storage] -m sr
```

Recovery with Local Storage

In the event recovery requires a reinstallation, consider that if the VM virtual disks reside on local storage, the option to create local storage during installation should be skipped.

Portable Storage Repositories

The most common storage repository used in XenServer is one that is fixed to either a host or a pool for the lifespan of the underlying storage. Portable storage repositories have sufficient information contained within them to allow all VMs contained in the repository to be attached to a new host or pool.

Problem

A full backup of all VMs on a storage repository is required.

Solution

A portable storage repository is an SR that has all necessary VM information to recreate those VMs on any XenServer pool. Portable SRs are particularly valuable during hardware upgrades where new pools are being created, but VM migration options like storage migration aren't an option.

In order to create a portable SR, the underlying virtual disk images must all reside on the same SR. A special backup disk is then created by XenSever that contains all metadata required to restore the VMs using that SR.

Discussion

The process of creating a portable SR is best done from within the XenServer command-line console, xsconsole, and must be done on the pool master. Example 10-8 shows the simple command to start xsconsole.

Example 10-8. Start xsconsole on the pool master

```
# xsconsole
```

Then select the option for "Backup, Restore and Update." We'll first start by creating a new backup for the desired storage by selecting "Backup Virtual Machine Metadata." Once complete, a portable SR has been created, but as new VMs are created and old ones retired, this data will become stale. To resolve this, define a schedule under "Schedule Virtual Machine Metadata." Create a schedule that matches the frequency VM metadata changes within that SR.

Restoring a portable SR in a new pool is easily accomplished by adding the portable SR to the new pool, starting xsconsole on the pool master, selecting "Backup, Restore and Update" and then choosing the portable SR from the list of storage options.

## CHAPTER 11

User Management

All XenServer installations come with a single predefined user, root. Because root is by definition a highly privileged user and provides access to services within the only privileged domain in a XenServer environment, it's very common for administrators to wish additional users be defined. In this chapter, we'll cover the concepts of Roles Based Authentication Controls (RBAC) and how they are used to provide granular user rights without granting everyone "root" access.

Dundee Changes

XenServer Dundee has shown a preview that includes a replacement for Likewise, which was used in XenServer 6.5 and prior. This replacement is known as Power-Broker Identity Services, or PBIS. More information on PBIS can be found at *http://www.powerbrokeropen.org/*.

Enabling Roles Based Authentication

Problem

A multiuser administration environment is desired.

Solution

XenServer has a rich roles-based administration environment suitable for most data center operations.

Discussion

After installation, the root user is the only user that exists for a XenServer. Regardless of other authentication methods, the root user account will always have access to XenServer via SSH, through XenCenter, or through other administration tools built on the Xen API. This is because root uses local authentication on a XenServer, not via any outside or third-party, user-based authentication.

Because the creation of additional user space accounts will result in their deletion on reboot, XenServer leverages Kerberos and Likewise for RBAC with Active Directory. This type of setup, or configuring role-based users off a third-party authentication system, is very important for one important reason. It prevents, especially in Xen-Server pool deployments, the need to ensure users are locally defined across a pool. By leveraging RBAC and Active Directory, the XenServer administrator has a single point where users, access levels, and so forth remain persistent to keep consistency. It also ensures the XenServer administrator can alter a user's access, or revoke it, from one source instead of many.

To leverage RBAC and Active Directory, the XenServer administrator has to ensure that the following prerequisites are met:

- Active Directory from Windows 2003 (or greater) is required.
- Kerberos must be enabled on the Active Directory.
  - Kerberos is used by XenServer, so this must be enabled.
- For XenServer hosts joining a specific domain, each XenServer hostname must be unique.
  - If two hostnames are the same and join the same domain, the second host will overwrite the first.
- Hostnames for XenServers must be alpha-numeric, no longer than 63 characters, and cannot be numeric only.
  - An example of a good XenServer hostname is: xshost001.
  - An example of a bad XenServer hostname is: 000000001.
- Active Directory and XenServers should use the same DNS servers and NTP servers.
- Ports 53, 88, 123, 137, 139, 389, 445, 464, and 3268 must be opened from Xen-Server, through firewalls, and to the AD server.
  - For information related to IPTABLES, please see the administration guide.
- Likewise follows the AD account renewal policy for passwords, such as documented here: *http://support.microsoft.com/kb/154501*.

It needs to be understood that once associated with a domain, only users configured within that domain for XenServer access can manage a host or pool. If users require SSH access, the Active Directory group for XenServer administration cannot have more than 500 users.

While external authentication is a "per-host" configuration, it is recommended to use the "pool-level" configuration to enable Active Directory authentication. The command in Example 11-1 should be issued from the XenServer pool master.

Example 11-1. Enable AD integration

```
# xe pool-enable-external-auth auth-type=AD \
  service-name=<full-qualified-domain> config:user=<username> \
  config:pass=<password>
```

Configuring Users

Problem

Users are unable to log in to XenServer after the pool has joined the domain.

Solution

Users requiring access to XenServer need to be added to the XenServer pool and assigned to specific roles.

Discussion

XenServer offers six different types of RBAC roles. These are documented within the administration guide and should be leveraged within Active Directory group configuration:

- Pool admin
  - The same level of access as root
- Pool operator
  - Can perform any action except user management
- VM power admin
  - VM creation and management
- VM admin
  - Cannot migrate VMs or make snapshots
- VM operator
  - Can perform VM stop/start functions
- Read only
  - Can only view resource data/metrics

Once a XenServer host or XenServer pool is associated with a domain, users are unable to log in until a subject is added to a user or group. To add an Active Directory subject for XenServer issue the command in Example 11-2.

Example 11-2. Add AD user or group

```
# xe subject-add subject-name=<entity name>
```

Removing Users

Problem

You wish to revoke access to a user or group of users.

Solution

Users having access to XenServer need to have that access revoked.

Discussion

To revoke access, first find the UUID of the subject by issuing the command in Example 11-3.

Example 11-3. Locate UUID of the subject

```
# xe subject-list
```

Then with the UUID known, issue the command in Example 11-4.

Example 11-4. Remove specific user or group

```
# xe subject-remove subject-name=<subject-uuid>
```

Disable External Authentication

Problem

The existing authentication provider needs to be replaced with an alternate.

Solution

The easiest way to accomplish this task is to remove the existing authentication provider and add in the new one. Care must be taken to ensure any objects associated with the previous authentication model are removed.

Discussion

First you will need to disable the existing authentication provider while logged in as "root," as shown in Example 11-5.

Example 11-5. Disable authentication provider

```
# xe pool-disable-external-auth
```

While this will leave the domain, it will not clear out host objects, etc. Refer to the following article, *http://support.microsoft.com/kb/197478*, to remove objects from the Active Directory database.

In order to remove existing object references, run the script in Example 11-6 on each host within the pool.

Example 11-6. Remove all AD references

```
#!/bin/bash
#
# resetAD.sh
# 2014-2015, Jesse Benedict
# Remove and clear Likewise configs
#

# Clear old domain config
rm -rf /var/lib/likewise
mkdir -p /var/lib/likewise/{db,rpc,run}
chmod 700 /var/lib/likewise/db

# Start services
/etc/init.d/lwsmd restart
for file in /etc/likewise/*.reg; do /opt/likewise/bin/lwregshell import $file; done
/etc/init.d/lwsmd reload
/etc/init.d/lsassd start
```

Privileged (Root) Password Recovery

Even if a XenServer or pooled XenServer deployment is configured to leverage Roles Based Access Control, *root* is still the active privileged account for access into dom0 user space. This includes direct console access, remote SSH access, or secured and "stunnel'd" access to the command line via XenCenter. While it is rare, the root password can be lost or forgotten.

Problem

The root password was forgotten and XenCenter is still active with a user having pool admin rights.

Solution

Access the host command line and reset the password.

Discussion

If XenCenter happens to be running and you have access to the XenServer command line, simply execute `passwd`. You will be prompted to create a new root user password and then prompted again to verify it, just like a standard Linux password reset. Exit out of XenCenter and attempt to reconnect to the host. A dialog should appear, stating that the password is incorrect. Simply enter in the new password and all is well.

Problem

The root user password was forgotten, and XenCenter isn't in use or otherwise active.

Solution

Because dom0 is Linux, standard Linux password recovery techniques can be used. In this case, we'll restart the host in single-user mode.

Discussion

If the XenServer host in question has a means of remote access, such as iLO, or if you have physical access to the XenServer host locally, single-user access will need to be gained. To accomplish this, first reboot the host. After the host completes post, the boot prompt shown in Figure 11-1 will appear for a few seconds. Type in `menu.c32` and press the Enter key immediately.

```
SYSLINUX 4.06 EDD 0x51a10931 Copyright (C) 1994-2012 H. Peter Anvin et al
boot: menu.c32_
```

Figure 11-1. Access boot menu

The `menu.c32` boot prompt will appear, and again, you will only have five or so seconds to select the "xe" entry and pressing Tab to edit boot options (see Figure 11-2).

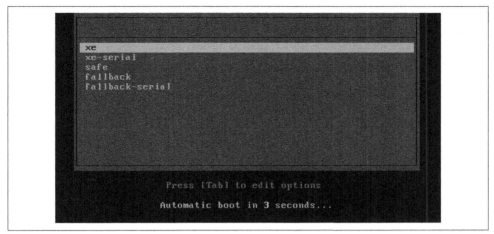

Figure 11-2. Specify startup configuration for boot

Now, at the bottom of the screen, you will see the boot entry information. Don't worry, unlike the initial boot, you have time to edit this command. Near the end of the boot command, you should see `console=tty0 quiet vga=785 splash quiet`, replace `quiet vga=785 splash` with `linux single`, as shown in Figure 11-3. More specifically, without the quotes, such as:

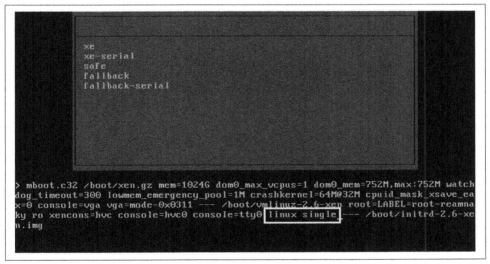

Figure 11-3. Specify Linux single-user mode for startup

With that completed, simply press Enter to boot into Linux's single-user mode. Once the boot process has completed, use the `passwd` command to create a new root password. With the new password set, reboot the host, and once dom0 access is visible, reconnect to the host via XenCenter and supply the new root user's password.

## CHAPTER 12

SSL Certificates

During the installation process, a self-signed SSL (Secure Socket Layer) certificate is generated for the XenServer host that is set to expire after 10 years. This is used for secure communications between the host and management tools, other XenServer hosts, or third-party software.

Reboot Required

If the default certificate for a XenServer host is going to be replaced or updated, it is recommended to reboot that XenServer host. Ensure that Guest VMs are halted or migrated to other hosts within a XenServer pool. Lastly, all administrators using XenCenter should expect, upon reconnecting to the XenServer host, a warning that there has been a change in the SSL Certificate/Trust. The administrator can accept this change to reestablish trust from from XenCenter to the host.

Apply a Commercial Certificate

Problem

A self-signed SSL certificate is not acceptable for your organization and a commercial one must be used.

Solution

XenServer supports the replacement of the default SSL certificate with a certified purchase through a trusted certificate authority (CA).

Discussion

In the process of obtaining a signed certificate from a trusted authority, you will need to generate a CSR (certificate signing request). This is generated along with your private key and is a block of text containing encrypted information about your company, location, and contact information for an administrator of the host. The CSR also allows the certificate authority to use this in the generation of a signed, trusted SSL certificate for your XenServer host without the need to exchange your private key.

To generate the CSR and private key for a specific XenServer host, issue the commands in Example 12-1 to store these in the */root/* directory.

Example 12-1. Producing myserver.csr in /root/

```
# cd /root/
# openssl req -new -nodes -keyout myserver.key \
-out myserver.csr \
-newkey rsa:2048
```

After sharing the *myserver.csr* file with a trusted authority, they will return to you a certificate and private key in PEM format. If you are unsure if this format is being followed, contact your trusted authority to confirm this before continuing.

With the signed certificate downloaded, use scp or any secure copy program to copy the certificate *.pem* file into the */tmp/* directory of your XenServer. Access the command line of the XenServer host. Back up the original self-signed certificate on the XenServer host by issuing the command in Example 12-2.

Example 12-2. Back up original SSL certificate

```
# mv /etc/xensource/xapi-ssl.pem \
/etc/xensource/xapi-ssl.pem_original
```

Move and rename your new *.pem* file, replacing the original with the code in Example 12-3.

Example 12-3. Replace original certificate and reset its permissions

```
# mv /tmp/your_certificate.pem /etc/xensource/xapi-ssl.pem
# chmod 400 /etc/xensource/xapi-ssl.pem
```

To apply the new certificate, reboot the XenServer host.

Create a New Self-Signed Certificate

Problem

An updated SSL certificate is required to address a potential security concern.

Solution

Create a new SSL certificate on the XenServer host.

Discussion

The following steps, executed from the XenServer host's command line, will generate a new certificate in the same manner the XenServer installer does. Because the XenServer installer uses a default of 10 years, or 3,650 days, we will also create a 10-year certificate. If a shorter amount of time is required, simply enter the number of days you would like the host's certificate to be valid, such as 365 (for one year).

Before proceeding, ensure that the current IP address of the XenServer's management interface is correct for production. If the IP address is changed later on, this will invalidate the certificate and the process will need to be repeated with the new IP.

A quick means to determine the management interface's IP address is shown in Example 12-4.

Example 12-4. Determine primary management IP

```
# ip addr show
1: lo: <LOOPBACK,UP,LOWER_UP> mtu 65536 qdisc noqueue
    state UNKNOWN
    link/loopback 00:00:00:00:00:00 brd 00:00:00:00:00:00
    inet 127.0.0.1/8 scope host lo
       valid_lft forever preferred_lft forever
7: xenbr0: <BROADCAST,UP,LOWER_UP> mtu 1500 qdisc noqueue
    state UNKNOWN
    link/ether b8:ac:6f:85:f4:91 brd ff:ff:ff:ff:ff:ff
    inet 10.0.0.20/8 brd 10.0.0.255 scope global xenbr0
       valid_lft forever preferred_lft forever
```

Execute the script in Example 12-5 to create the new SSL certificate where the CN (certificate name) is set to the primary management IP.

Example 12-5. Create new certificate

```
# cd ~
# mkdir cert
# cd cert/
# openssl req -x509 -nodes -days 3650 -subj '/CN=10.0.1.20' \
  -newkey rsa:1024 -keyout new-ssl.pem -out new-ssl.pem
# openssl dhparam 512 >> new-ssl.pem
```

Execute the script in Example 12-6 to replace the original SSL certificate with this new certificate.

Example 12-6. Replace original SSL certificate

```
# mv /etc/xensource/xapi-ssl.pem /root/cert/xapi-ssl.pem_original
# mv /root/cert/new-ssl.pem /etc/xensource/xapi-ssl.pem
# chmod 400 /etc/xensource/xapi-ssl.pem
```

Once complete, reboot the XenServer host to load the new certificate.

## CHAPTER 13

Hardware Maintenance

Once deployed, it's not uncommon for XenServer installations to run without incident for years. Often, it's a hardware issue or growth in requirements that prompts administrators to look at their XenServer infrastructure. In this chapter, we'll be covering practices for everything related to hardware maintenance, be it storage, network, or computer.

Upgrades, Support, and Hardware

A chapter on hardware wouldn't be complete without some discussion of how the XenServer hardware compatibility list (HCL) works. As mentioned in Chapter 4, the XenServer HCL is located at *http://hcl.xenserver.org*. A component gets added to the HCL when the hardware vendor and Citrix agree that they will jointly accept user support calls for a given version of XenServer on that hardware.

While in a perfect world, all hardware would be tested and certified for new versions, the reality is that often, hardware vendors wish to no longer certify XenServer for legacy or end-of-life hardware. This doesn't mean XenServer won't function on older hardware, but if you want to maintain a "supported platform" in the eyes of Citrix and your hardware vendor, you may find that upgrading XenServer past a certain version will place you into "unsupported" territory.

As a XenServer administrator, it's important to pay attention to the HCL as you plan out your upgrades. Newer hardware may not have been certified for older versions of XenServer, and older hardware may no longer be actively supported for newer versions of XenServer. If you find yourself in a situation where the hardware you wish to use isn't on the XenServer HCL, you should first start with your hardware vendor and determine if it is in the process of certification. Once the hardware vendor performs its certification, it then provides Citrix with the results, which Citrix then posts. By starting with the hardware vendor, you not only provide it with information about how its hardware is being used, but also might be able to add weight to any efforts that increase the priority of future XenServer certifications.

Storage

Each recipe in this section will relate to ensuring you have sufficient free storage to operate the XenServer pool at peak efficiency.

Adding Local Storage

Problem

As part of your XenServer design, you are using local storage for virtual machine disks. The usage requirements for those virtual machines require additional storage.

Solution

Assuming your server has sufficient free drive bays to install additional storage, you can add drives and within XenServer create new local storage repositories.

Changing the Default Local Storage

When XenServer is installed, it uses the existing drive for both dom0 and as local storage. Changing the physical configuration of that default drive will require a complete reinstall of XenServer.

Discussion

As the XenServer deployment grows, so will the need for storage and networking. When dealing with local storage, additional drives can be added; however, they have to be added to the host as "local storage 2," and so forth. As an example, if a 2.2 TB or greater capacity spindle drive is added to the host, on reboot, XenServer will not automatically pick this up. In the following sequence, we'll be adding a 4 TB drive as additional local storage.

While in the control domain, the drive will follow Linux conventions: being mapped to a device, such as /dev/sdb, and should be verified as being the large spindle drive that was added by issuing the command in Example 13-1.

Example 13-1. Checking the geometry of device /dev/sdb

```
# fdisk -l /dev/sdb
```

Because the drive is known to be 4 TB in size, if /dev/sdb is the device entry within the control domain for this spindle drive, fdisk should return an warning followed by the geometry of /dev/sdb and what the limit is for a DOS partition table format (2.2 TB), as shown in Example 13-2.

Example 13-2. Using fdisk to validate /dev/sdb

```
# fdisk -l /dev/sdb
WARNING: GPT (GUID Partition Table) detected on '/dev/sdb'!
The util fdisk doesn't support GPT. Use GNU Parted.
Note: sector size is 4096 (not 512)

WARNING: The size of this disk is 4.0 TB (4000787025920 bytes).
DOS partition table format can not be used on drives for volumes
larger than 2.2 TB (2199023255040 bytes). Use parted(1) and GUID
partition table format (GPT).

Disk /dev/sdb: 4000.7 GB, 4000787025920 bytes
255 heads, 63 sectors/track, 60800 cylinders
Units = cylinders of 16065 * 4096 = 65802240 bytes
Device Boot Start End Blocks Id System
/dev/sdb1 1 60801 3907018576 ee EFI GPT
```

Because we have confirmed device /dev/sdb is greater than 2.2 TB, fdisk cannot be used. The control domain offers gdisk to create GPT partitions for partitions less or greater than 2.2 TB; however, this is not necessary because XAPI can be used to accomplish this.

To add /dev/sdb as "local storage 2," the command in Example 13-3 can be issued on the XenServer host so it is formatted, checked, tagged with a UUID, and added to the XAPI database—appearing in XenCenter as a storage repository from this point out for the particular XenServer host.

Example 13-3. Create new local storage SR

```
# xe sr-create content-type=user device-config:device=/dev/sdb \
    host-uuid=<host-uuid> name-label="Local Storage 2" \
    shared=false type=lvm
```

Software RAID Configurations

XenServer doesn't support the use of software RAID configurations. If you wish to use multiple disks in a local SR, specify each disk in comma-separated format as part of the device-config parameter when creating the SR.

USB Storage for Backup

Problem

You wish to back up virtual machine disks onto removable media.

Solution

Removable media is automatically identified by XenServer and can be used for multiple purposes including as VM storage. In this example, we wish to use USB storage to back up virtual machines.

Discussion

XenServer also has support for udev, or USB-based devices. It is recommended these be used for backups and not actual VM disk storage. In my own experience, any USB flash or spindle device that is above 32 GB should be preformatted, outside of XenServer, with an EXT3 filesystem. The reason for this is that most types of such devices are NTFS-based. We want to ensure this drive is clean before plugging it in and determining its /dev/sdXY entry.

So, if I have a 4 TB volume attached to /dev/sde, I would execute the command in Example 13-4 to create a USB-based device to export backups to—allowing it to be disconnected from XenServer and reattached as needed.

Example 13-4. Create local storage SR for backup purposes

```
# xe sr-create content-type=user device-config:device=/dev/sde \
  host-uuid=<host-uuid> name-label="USB BACKUP" shared=false type=ext
```

Networking

Replacing a NIC

Problem

A network card has become defective and must be replaced.

Solution

Place the XenServer host into maintenance mode and replace the physical NIC, then configure XenServer to use the new NIC in place of the old NIC.

Discussion

During the installation or upgrade of XenServer, the host machine's hardware is profiled and stored in the XAPI database for dom0. This information is highly detailed to ensure that after installation and subsequent reboots for maintenance, the host's hardware is still in exact working order. This means that the administrator or IT department cannot just shut down a XenServer host: removing the faulty card and replacing it as if something has been changed on the host (such as a network card), or if it fails to load, then dom0 will run in a default "maintenance" mode where manual intervention is required.

An example of the type of information stored for a network card is shown in Example 13-5.

Example 13-5. NIC information

```
<row ref="OpaqueRef:028983cc-d0f7-316e-1d99-c822e3439f91"
__ctime="314225446"
__mtime="314225446"
DNS="10.0.0.2,10.0.0.3"
IP="10.0.0.10" IPv6="('')"
MAC="f0:92:1c:13:b7:08"
MTU="1500"
VLAN="-1" VLAN_master_of="OpaqueRef:NULL" VLAN_slave_of="()"
_ref="OpaqueRef:028983cc-d0f7-316e-1d99-c822e3439f91"
bond_master_of="('OpaqueRef:6a2b5648-af19-5636-5695-3e5385d0a81e')"
bond_slave_of="OpaqueRef:NULL" currently_attached="true"
device="bond0"
device_name="bond0"
disallow_unplug="false"
gateway="10.0.0.1"
host="OpaqueRef:1b25f88f-3c25-05c6-c00e-37859fd68ed4"
ip_configuration_mode="Static"
ipv6_configuration_mode="None"
ipv6_gateway=""
managed="true"
management="true"
metrics="OpaqueRef:d3d5e33f-a9b4-363e-1d9e-78b2ddc73f2d"
netmask="255.0.0.0" network="OpaqueRef:471f9e43-5d50-f525-dbbc-6ae1c10e462a"
other_config="()"
physical="false"
primary_address_type="IPv4"
tunnel_access_PIF_of="()"
tunnel_transport_PIF_of="()"
uuid="eda9c065-7bf6-ff9f-dc40-2ae53efc12c9"/>
```

By replacing the card without following the proper steps for a standalone host or pool, this information is now invalidated.

First we place the host into maintenance mode:

```
# xe host-disable
```

Then, if the NIC is a management interface, we need to disable it:

```
# xe host-management-disable
```

Next we determine the `pif` and find the device position for the NIC:

```
# xe pif-list params=all
```

Armed with the `pif`, we need to instruct XAPI to forget about it, and then the host must be halted and the replacement NIC installed:

```
# xe pif-forget uuid={pif-uuid}
# halt
```

After installing the new NIC and restarting the host, determine the MAC address for the replacement NIC:

```
# ip addr
```

We now need to introduce the replacement `pif` in the same position as the original. This requires the original device position and the new MAC address:

```
# xe pif-introduce device={device position} host-uuid={host-uuid} mac={new MAC}
```

With the `pif` defined, we can now add in any fixed network address parameters:

```
# xe pif-reconfigure-ip uuid={host-uuid} IP="10.0.0.20" \
netmask="255.0.0.0." gateway="10.0.0.1" dns="10.0.0.1"
```

and complete the task by reconfiguring the management network to use the new `pif` (assuming the original `pif` was a management network):

```
# xe host-management-reconfigure pif-uuid={pif-uuid}
```

Hosts

Adding a New Host to a Pool

Problem

The existing pool capacity is insufficient, and a new host needs to be added to the pool.

Solution

Obtain a host with comparable capabilities as the original host, and prepare to add it to the pool.

Discussion

As discussed earlier, resource pools provide an aggregate virtualization environment consisting of multiple hosts. In order to function at peak efficiency, the capabilities of each host should be as close as possible. This compatibility extends to the host CPU feature set, which should, ideally, be identical. Unfortunately, while processor vendors market a CPU as identical, individual steppings of a given processor may contain hardware fixes making them not quite identical.

While XenServer does a good job of masking CPU features, or ensuring that one host does not expose a CPU feature that other pool members do not have, this essentially diminishes the performance of the new host. Because operating systems are fully aware of the capabilities of a host CPU, it is imperative all CPUs in a resource pool have identical features lest the operating system crash in the event a VM migration occurs.

Don't Forget About Network Configuration

While CPU compatibility is paramount, it's important to recall that all hosts in a resource pool must have identical physical network configurations.

The first step in ensuing a consistent pool is to obtain the current features of the pool master:

```
# xe host-get-cpu-features
```

Copy the returned feature set and attempt to apply it to the new host prior to any attempt at joining the new host to the pool:

```
# xe host-set-cpu-features features=[pool master CPU features]
```

If successful, reboot the host and add it to the resource pool. In the event the command fails, this typically means the CPU doesn't adequately support feature masking. To verify this, you can obtain CPU information and compare it to the CPU information from the pool master, as shown in Example 13-6. If the "maskable" flag is set to anything other than "full," you may not be able to create a viable feature mask for this CPU.

Example 13-6. Determine CPU information

```
# xe host-cpu-info
```

Recovery from Host Failure When HA Is Enabled

Problem

Host failure occurred while the host was accessing the heartbeat state file, and the file has an orphaned lock.

Solution

To remove all locks, you must perform an emergency HA reset.

Discussion

If a partial host failure occurs while the HA daemon on the host was accessing the state file on shared storage, it may be necessary to temporarily disable HA. This can be done using the following command:

```
# xe host-emergency-ha-disable --force
```

If the host was a pool master, then it should automatically recover, and member servers should automatically reconnect. If a member server does not automatically reconnect, it may be necessary to reset the pool master address. This can be done using the following command on the impacted member server:

Reset pool master address on member server

```
# xe pool-emergency-reset-master master-address={pool_master_address}
```

Index

networks
monitoring, 13
objects representing, 24-26
topologies for, 58-62
types of, 24
virtual network fabric for, 20, 25
NFS (Network File System) storage, 45, 56
NIC bonding, 25, 59-61
NICs
replacing, 116-118
virtual, 25
ntp.conf file, 22

O

objects, 23-27
GPU objects, 26-27
network objects, 24-26
storage objects, 27
UUIDs for, 23
Open-iSCSI, 18
OpenStack, 40
openvswitch network, 20
ovs (Open Virtual Switch), 25

P

para-virtualized (PV) guests, 63, 64
patches (see upgrades)
PBD (physical block device), 27, 57
PBIS (PowerBroker Identity Services), 101
perfmon process, 13
performance
hardware affecting, 41
jumbo frames affecting, 61
memory configuration affecting, 48
monitoring, 13
PV drivers affecting, 64
storage media affecting, 29, 46
pGPU (physical Graphical Processor Unit), 26
pGPU object, 26
physical block device (PBD), 27, 57
pif object, 24
Pool Admin role, 103
Pool Operator role, 103
pool.conf file, 21
pooled hosts, 35-39
adding hosts to a pool, 38, 118-119
configuration of, backup and restore, 95
CPU compatibility within, 37-38
maximum number of hosts, 39

multiple pools, 24
resource pool sizing, 38
types of, 21, 36-37
when to create a new pool, 39
portable SRs, backups on, 99-99
portable storage repositories (SRs), backups on
PowerBroker Identity Services (PBIS), 101
Primary Management network, 24
privileged domains, 9
(see also dom0)
processes (see core processes)
processors (see CPUs)
provisioning tools, 40
ptoken file, 21
PV (para-virtualized) guests, 63, 64
PVHVM, 64
PXE-based installation (see installation: unattended)

Q

QEMU (Quick Emulator), 9-10

R

RAID configurations, software, 115
RBAC (Roles Based Authentication Controls),
102, 103
(see also Active Directory)
Read Only role, 103
resiliency (see infrastructure failure planning)
resolv.conf file, 17
resource pool sizing, 38
roles based authentication, 101-103
(see also Active Directory)
root password recovery, 105-108
root user, 101
round-robin database, 12

S

safe label, 15
SAN, boot from, 32, 71-72
scripts directory, 21
Secure Shell (SSH) access to CLI, 10
security
patches for, 78
roles based authentication, 101-103
secure tunnel, 14
SSL certificate, commercial, 109-110
SSL certificate, self-signed, 109, 111-112

About the Authors

When **Tim Mackey** isn't tinkering with code or helping to solve some technical issue, he can be found speaking at various technology events the world over. That in itself is truly just the tip of the iceberg in trying to describe Tim's expansive role and travels. Truly, his schedule is so hectic at times that we have played "Where's Tim?" in homage to Waldo (minus the stripes, naturally) and over various media! While almost always available despite being one of the busiest, tech-passionate individuals we know, what I think we all love most about Tim is his warm, humble, and passionate approach to all projects and individuals he is involved with. In between this and that, when Tim has downtime between events and work, you're most likely to find him playing something with his wonderful son, Liam.

If you are looking for Tim online, he can be found at:

- Twitter: @XenServerArmy (*https://twitter.com/XenServerArmy*)
- SlideShare: *http://slideshare.net/TimMackey*
- LinkedIn: *https://www.linkedin.com/in/mackeytim*

As for **Jesse Benedict**, when he isn't spending sleepless nights on items he and Tim are working on, tinkering with virtualizing exotic operating systems, or writing code on archaic hardware, he can be found at home with his true passion: being a husband to his wonderful wife, Melissa, and a father to their boys, Maddox and Trent. Both he and his younger brother, David, were exposed to music and computers during their youth, and the latter became careers, thanks to their father, Mark. After many years being an architect and developer—and wearing many other hats with various titles—he has been quite content with a return to the technology behind virtualization that has fascinated him since his youth. This field of work is what both Jesse and Tim live for: especially in sharing what they know to those who helped push their own success.

If you are looking for Jesse, he can be found at the various haunts listed here:

- XenServer.org: *http://xenserver.org/blog/blogger/listings/xenfomation.html*
- Twitter: @Xenfomation (*https://twitter.com/Xenfomation*)
- Personal: *http://xenfomation.wordpress.com*
- Citrix: *https://www.citrix.com/blogs/author/jessebe*

Colophon

The animal on the cover of *XenServer Administration Handbook* is a plain xenops (*Xenops minutus*). It is part of the Furnariidae family and can be found throughout the rainforests of Central and South America, as well as Mexico. They are also known as "ovenbirds."

Both males and females have a similar look, but immature xenopses have dark brown throats. Adults are fairly small, weighing an average of 12 grams and measuring about 12 centimeters in length. Plummage on the heads is a light brown, with an even lighter stripe that starts from the base of the bill, extends above the eye, and ends toward the back of the head. Their "cheeks" also include a lighter-colored strip of plummage. The rest of the body is also of a brown color, but turns slightly reddish toward the tail. Wings are of a darker shade of brown than the upper parts.

The plain xenops' diet relies heavily on insects (namely ants) and their larvae caught within decaying tree and shrub branches. The bird is sometimes hard to spot as it moves in all directions on tree trunks, in search of its next meal.

When breeding, both male and female plain xenops create a nest between 1.5 and 9 meters off the ground, within a tree trunk or branch in decay. Both sexes also take turns in incubating the eggs. Each female averages two eggs per breeding.

Many of the animals on O'Reilly covers are endangered; all of them are important to the world. To learn more about how you can help, go to animals.oreilly.com.

The cover image is from *Shaw's Zoology*. The cover fonts are URW Typewriter and Guardian Sans. The text font is Adobe Minion Pro; the heading font is Adobe Myriad Condensed; and the code font is Dalton Maag's Ubuntu Mono.

Get even more for your money.

Join the O'Reilly Community, and register the O'Reilly books you own. It's free, and you'll get:

- $4.99 ebook upgrade offer
- 40% upgrade offer on O'Reilly print books
- Membership discounts on books and events
- Free lifetime updates to ebooks and videos
- Multiple ebook formats, DRM FREE
- Participation in the O'Reilly community
- Newsletters
- Account management
- 100% Satisfaction Guarantee

Signing up is easy:

1. Go to: oreilly.com/go/register
2. Create an O'Reilly login.
3. Provide your address.
4. Register your books.

Note: English-language books only

To order books online:
oreilly.com/store

For questions about products or an order:
orders@oreilly.com

To sign up to get topic-specific email announcements and/or news about upcoming books, conferences, special offers, and new technologies:
elists@oreilly.com

For technical questions about book content:
booktech@oreilly.com

To submit new book proposals to our editors:
proposals@oreilly.com

O'Reilly books are available in multiple DRM-free ebook formats. For more information:
oreilly.com/ebooks

Lightning Source UK Ltd.
Milton Keynes UK
UKOW05f1838070616

275793UK00004B/16/P